T0357532

FACING DOWN
THE FURIES

FACING DOWN THE FURIES

THE FURIES

SUICIDE, THE ANCIENT

GREEKS, AND ME

EDITH HALL

Yale

UNIVERSITY PRESS

NEW HAVEN & LONDON

Published with assistance from the Louis Stern Memorial Fund.

Yale University Press books may be purchased in quantity for
educational, business, or promotional use. For information,
please e-mail sales.press@yale.edu (U.S. office) or
sales@yaleup.co.uk (U.K. office).

Set in Spectral and Shango type by IDS Infotech Ltd.
Printed in the United States of America.

Library of Congress Control Number: 2023941992
ISBN 978-0-300-27353-3 (hardcover : alk. paper)

A catalogue record for this book is available from the British Library.

This paper meets the requirements of ANSI/NISO Z39.48-1992
(Permanence of Paper).

10 9 8 7 6 5 4 3 2 1

Our deeds are like children that are born to us; they live and act apart from our will; nay, children may be strangled, but deeds never; they have an indestructible life, both in and out of our consciousness.

—George Eliot

Contents

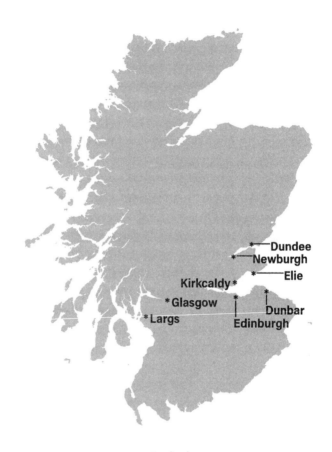

Scotland

FACING DOWN
THE FURIES

Introduction

Suicide is an event of human nature which, whatever may be
said and done with respect to it, demands the sympathy
of every man, and in every epoch must be discussed anew.
—Goethe, *Truth and Poetry*

A FEW YEARS AGO I PUBLISHED A BOOK ABOUT
Aristotle in which I argued that his philosophy, especially his
works on ethics and politics, offers a practical guide to self-scru-
tiny and to developing habits that can lead to a more contented
life—and death. Several people have since written to me com-
menting that, in writing about how to achieve a happy way of life,
which requires mental energy and commitment to the project, I
seemed to have glossed over the problems posed by severe depression; my only relevant observation in that book was that there are
times when modern antidepressants, which enhance the levels of
serotonin, can benefit people who are either experiencing temporary grief as a reaction to a life event, or suffering from "endogenous," persistent depression.[1] No amount of moral philosophy
can alleviate deep despair.

The inquiries have made me acutely aware that in writing
about living my life according to Aristotle's prescriptions for happiness, I had indeed evaded talking about my own confrontations
with depression and even, as a young adult, battles with suicidal
urges. I am also painfully aware of the number of people affected
by suicide worldwide.

Knowing that any individual has deliberately chosen death
by suicide is always difficult for others to bear. When it is an
individual whom we loved, admired, or were dependent on, the

suicide brings a special burden of agony, as well, often, as embarrassment or shame, on top of the loss, feelings that exacerbate the simple fact of bereavement. In Sophocles' tragedy *Oedipus the Tyrant,* for example, a messenger arrives to report that Jocasta, queen of Thebes, has killed herself, and in trying to prepare his listeners for the terrible news, he notes, "The tragedies that hurt the most are those that the sufferers have chosen for themselves."

This book is about my family, particularly my mother and grandmother, both of whom lived for decades under the shadow of a parent's decision to die by suicide and the "successful" implementation of that decision. But the book is also about how ancient Greek literature, especially Greek tragedy, has helped me understand the damage caused by suicide and has eased my matrilineally inherited burden of psychological pain. I hope it will help others who have suffered from the intergenerational impact of this saddest way of dying, as well as those in such despair that they are contemplating suicide themselves.

When I have referred to my own experience of ancestral suicide—which I do in conversation even with recent acquaintances as part of my attempt to correct the silence and stigma surrounding the subject—I have been staggered by the number of people whose eyes have welled up, as they confide in me, often overcoming acute embarrassment and shame, how the self-killing of friends or family members—parents, siblings, children, aunts and uncles, grandparents, cousins, or even more distant relatives—has affected them.

In the autumn of 2021, five years after my own mother's death at the age of ninety from natural causes, I began a long-postponed investigation into the lives of my suicidal ancestors, about whom I knew very little. In the summer of 2022 this culminated in a journey across southern Scotland, where they had lived and died. The investigation, the journey, and in particular leaving flowers at the sites where these ancestors had taken their own lives have brought me overwhelming relief. This book is in part an account of my melancholy but ultimately constructive adventure.

A motive in writing it was to track down one source of my own problems—the history of suicide in my maternal family tree. A second motive was to contribute to the secular philosophical case against suicide, a position so passionately articulated in Jennifer Michael Hecht's *Stay: A History of Suicide and the Arguments Against It* (2013). She wrote this book in a state of despondency after two of her female friends killed themselves. Despite her own bereavements, however, Hecht did not stress the personal trauma inflicted on individuals by suicide. Her emphasis was on our broader obligation to the rest of humanity to stay alive.

Her case seems to have its roots in the somewhat obscure pronouncement of the medieval Jewish sage Moses Maimonides, "He who destroys himself destroys the world." She also explains lucidly Immanuel Kant's view in *Groundwork for the Metaphysics of Morals* (1785), deriving from his concept of the Categorical Imperative, that the effect of suicide, if everybody carried it out, would be to extinguish the very subject of morality itself, humanity. She does point out that Kant also opens this discussion with the far less grand-sounding objection to suicide that almost all of us owe it to some other individual to stay alive.[2] But the purely secular moral case against suicide, although still underdeveloped today, was in fact initiated by Aristotle: suicide wrongs other people.

Its collateral, indeed transgenerational damage has until recently received minimal attention in any medium or cultural arena. But there is one shining exception. In ancient Greek tragedy, first performed two and a half millennia ago, the impact of suicide on parents, children, spouses, friends, dependents, and citizens was explored in painful, illuminating, and impressively nonjudgmental detail. A third objective of mine here was therefore to describe how reading these tragedies helped me understand the causes of suicide and especially its effects on those left behind. I am convinced that intensive reading of Greek tragedy helped save my own life when I was a young adult, and it has informed my responses to suicide ever since. The tragedians left extraordinary scenes in which anguished people talk about suicide, die by suicide, are sometimes talked out of suicide, and above all, if they are not, are lamented bitterly by their families, friends, and communities. There is much wisdom in these scenes. Scholars of faith have researched the therapeutic potential for coping with mental health problems that can be discovered in biblical narratives. Greek tragedies largely take divinity out of the moral equation, and therefore may be able to speak to humanity more widely.[3] I hope that my exploration of them, together with my own family history of suicide, can be of some benefit to others.

Chapter 1

BEGINNING THE JOURNEY: ANCESTRAL CURSES

IT WAS A SUNNY AUTUMN DAY IN 2021 WHEN I AND my two adult children arrived at the house where my mother had spent her childhood summer holidays. We clambered out of the hired van and knocked on the old, white-painted door. The air smelt tangy from the nearby harbor, and the seagulls were in noisy altercation. The solid Victorian house, squatting behind straggly rosebushes, was where my mother had spent the happiest days of her childhood and, with my father, the last three decades of her adult life. My sister Nicky, three years older than I, had now moved in with her husband. The house seemed smaller and more dilapidated than I remembered. My stomach was churning and my tear ducts prickling. I had crossed the threshold only twice, and then briefly, since my mother's death in July 2016.

Less than two hours later we drove off, the van jammed with books, pictures, crockery, and furniture which my sister did not want or that I had asked for. I was delighted with one enormous, beautiful tapestry of medieval design. It depicts, in bright woolen stitches, Cecilia, the patron saint of music. She plays an organ in a sylvan setting. My mother was a phenomenal needlewoman, and for reasons I do not know had said she wanted me to inherit her masterpiece.

Leaning beside it in the van was another, far more delicate piece of needlework. It was a framed picture, done in tiny gold, cream, pink, and beige silk embroidery stitches, of a woman in late eighteenth-century costume weeping at a tomb. The oval picture is framed by a border depicting a variety of foliage, requiring the most intricate needlework. The romantic backdrop suggests the high trees of a cemetery. I did not know the identity of the forlorn, weeping woman, but I had always admired her flowing gown and mournful beauty. I was pleased that my sister let me have her. Our mother had told me that the piece was the work of *her* mother, Edith Henderson, née Masterton, after whom I had been named.

When we arrived home in Cambridgeshire and the two pictures had been fixed to the sitting-room wall, I felt a wave of pleasure. These two women, Edith and her daughter Brenda, had dominated my internal thought world for my entire life. My mother had been visiting me almost nightly in distressing dreams ever since her death, sometimes accompanied by *her* mother. Despite incessant and assiduous introspection (assisted by an online therapist during the Covid-19 lockdown), I had been unable to work out why.

I hoped that I could be helped by the domestic presence of these two comforting works of art, one of which shows a woman singing and the other a woman sobbing. They seemed to affirm the presence of my foremothers in my mind. Perhaps now these ancestors would live with me in my home as figures less sorrowfully spectral and more warmly benign. After all, these artworks had cost their makers hundreds of hours of concentration and handiwork, conscientiously creating beauty with their needles, tiny craft scissors, and colored skeins.

As we unloaded the van I came across one item that gave me less pleasure. A large, crumbling box of corrugated cardboard was full of old photographs and papers. I put it on my mother's mahogany dining-room table, which we had just reassembled in its new home, and picked out the top picture. I instantly realized that this box had emotionally explosive potential. The photograph included my grandmother as a young woman. I knew that she was a superb embroiderer, that she had once studied and taught English literature, that her father, Robert, had killed himself, and that she had followed suit on October 1, 1962. But I knew little else about her.

The picture at the top of the box was taken, according to a note inscribed on its back, in 1912. It is a formal photograph of a group of young people in Edwardian clothing topped with academic gowns, posing as if to signal their gravitas and intelligence as they gaze out at the camera. They are all men except for the young woman, Edith Masterton, sitting at the lower left-hand corner. The printed title reads, "STUDENTS' REPRESENTA-TIVE COUNCIL, Executive Committee, 1911–12." I now know that the photograph must have been taken at Edinburgh University during the academic year just before Edith's father drowned himself. She looks inquisitive, poised, self-possessed—and alone.

Looking at the photograph, I felt pride, confusion, and sudden grief in equal measure. This was the woman my mother obdurately refused to talk about all her life except to tell me that I was "just like her" and that she regretted giving me her name. Edith Masterton, however, had calmly joined the student council at a prestigious and ancient university years before she or any other British woman was even allowed to vote. Had she put herself forward for election? Had she been nominated by her peers, either women or men? Had she achieved anything that helped change the situation of students at Edinburgh University during those tense prewar years? Did she feel isolated at the council meetings? Had those young, self-confident men treated her with respect and friendliness, or condescension and distance? Was she in love with any of them, or they with her? How many of them had survived the imminent, cataclysmic war that killed hundreds of thousands of northwestern Europe's young men, or the deadly influenza epidemic that followed so closely on its heels? And why

"Students' Representative Council, Executive Committee, 1911–12."
(Photographer unknown, author's collection.)

had my mother never shown me the picture, even when I went to university myself? It might have given me some perspective later. She could have shown it to me when I complained to her about finding myself the only woman present in countless seminars and professional meetings, especially early in my academic working life.

But on this day I could not bear the sight of it. I was already emotionally exhausted from my return to that eastern Scottish house of memories and secrets and by the long drive home. I put the lid back on the box and asked my husband to stow it safely in the garage. This Pandora's box could wait for another day.

But of course putting the box out of sight in the garage did not prevent a flood of memories of my own childhood and family from pouring into my consciousness over the weeks that followed. I do have a few grainy memories of my grandmother. In one, she is sitting looking pensive at the left of the high marble mantelpiece in the drawing room of a substantial residence. This was an imposing bourgeois mansion on a sweeping boulevard in the spacious garden suburb of Pollokshields, Glasgow Southside. She shared it with her husband, my grandfather Walter Henderson, a prosperous Glasgow solicitor.

In another, more impressionistic and sensual memory, she is failing to teach me to write the alphabet in a dark-navy hardback notebook. We are sitting on deckchairs in a warm summer garden. She smells of lavender, and the sun is slanting through her wavy hair. I could not have been more than three and a half.

I can be certain that I was no older than that because the event which has marked my entire psychological development occurred on October 1, 1962, half a year after my third birthday. I was sitting on the floor of the front room downstairs in a house I now know was 98 North Road, West Bridgford, Nottingham. I was playing contentedly with some wooden bricks. I was alone with my mother, who was sitting on a sofa reading a broadsheet newspaper, as she often did.

The phone rang in the hall. (Domestic phones were always located in the hall in 1962.) My next recollection is of bellowing. I could hear my mother bellowing, first in the hall, then upstairs. It was a loud contralto sound, straight from the guts. I can remember being alarmed but deciding not to go after her. So I stayed sitting among my bricks. When she returned, after what felt like a long time, she grabbed me, clutched me to her, and kept croaking, "O Edith, Edith." Her face was wet.

I don't remember what happened next. My parents disappeared for many days, and I do recall missing my mother. Nobody talked about the reason for her disappearance. It was years before I was told that my grandmother was dead, and even longer before I knew that she had killed herself. I spent at least some of these days or weeks in late 1962 staying, along with my older brother and my sister, with a family who were friends of my parents. The father, like mine, was an ordained priest in the Church of England, the mother a kind, bustling woman whose cooking I enjoyed immensely. This couple had four small children of comparable ages to ours, and it was an act of huge generosity on their part to take in three more. I can only assume that my father, who had just that autumn taken up a lectureship in theology at Nottingham University, had been unable to cope with being left alone with us. I have later learned that he did return from Scotland well before my mother, but he did not retrieve his children until she reappeared.

That is almost the complete extent of my own memories connected with Edith Henderson, née Masterton. Over the subsequent five decades I tried to find out more about her. My mother eventually told me that she had been "troubled" and "troublesome," subject to depression her whole life, and that she had deliberately jumped out of the window of a hotel at a seaside resort on the west coast of Scotland. There were several people in her family background who suffered from depression or alcoholism, or who died by suicide, but my mother would get upset if she spoke about them.

She always started to cry when I probed for more information, so eventually I gave up. But my mother was always, as far as I was concerned, someone who had been deeply damaged by her mother's death and inexplicably seemed to associate me more than my siblings with that damage. Consequently, in a mysterious way that I aim to investigate in this book, the damage was passed on to me.

◊ ◊ ◊

Since my early teens, I have spent my life reading and finding comfort (as well as intellectual stimulation and aesthetic pleasure) in the works of the ancient Greeks. Their philosophers conducted an intense investigation into the morality of what they called *autothanasia,* "bringing death on oneself." Their tragedians depict several suicides, some of them of mothers, and detail the painful effects on both the community and the bereaved family members who survive. Perhaps the ancient Greeks' fascination with people who kill themselves—the Germans candidly call the act *Selbstmord,* "self-murder"—was one reason why I ended up teaching ancient Greek as a profession. Perhaps it is also why I have published more than a dozen books on Greek tragedy, and have been a consultant on so many productions of these timeless dramas, both professional and amateur. Over the past year, I have gone farther, turning to the ancient Greeks for help in escaping the lasting impact, handed on to me by my mother despite her best efforts, of *her* mother's—my grandmother's—suicide.[1]

I would never have become a classicist had I not fallen in love with the ancient Greeks at school. The Romans and the Latin language never inspired me in the same way. And it was by a fortunate accident of history that I learned ancient Greek as a teenager. In this beautiful language were written what I still maintain, despite risking accusations of Eurocentrism, are some of the greatest literary and philosophical works in the world. Sadly, ancient Greek has rarely been available to British children outside private schools. But the Butler Education Act of 1944 made it possible for children who passed the controversial "Eleven-Plus" examination (which selected the top 25 percent of children, supposedly on intellectual merit, at the age of eleven) to win publicly funded places at fee-paying schools. So instead of at a secondary modern school (for the 75 percent of students deemed less academically able and unlikely to extend their education beyond the statutory minimum school-leaving age of sixteen), I studied at the selective Nottingham Girls' High School, a "Direct Grant" school equivalent to a boys' grammar school (where most pupils continued their education to eighteen years old and progressed to a university).

I attended alongside girls from prosperous and aspirational families who paid tuition; they made up 40 percent of the student body. But I was one of the 60 percent of pupils who had succeeded in the Eleven-Plus, and we were drawn from a wide cross-section of the Nottinghamshire population. This cohort included some girls from very disadvantaged families and some from mining communities. The divisive grammar-school system was phased out in most of England in the mid-1970s, so I was one of the last of the selected few directly to experience its social engineering.

My father and my older brother and sister had all studied Classics at some point, and it was virtually assumed that at the age of fourteen I would begin to study for the Greek O-level exam. Since I did not particularly enjoy Latin—the first author we read was Julius Caesar, who spent a lot of time drearily detailing his own endless and brutal military successes—I was not all that keen. But I absolutely delighted in Greek, with its long polysyllabic nouns, riotous irregular verbs, and nuanced moods and voices, offering far more variety of self-expression than modern English, let alone Latin. Greek is also the vehicle for some of the richest myths and most searing emotional honesty in the cultural repertoire of the world.

The decisive moment came when we started reading our first prescribed text, Euripides' intensely poetic but emotionally bleak tragedy *Iphigenia in Aulis.* A brutal militaristic king, Agamemnon, decides, based on an oracle, that his innocent teenage daughter Iphigenia, his oldest child, must be sacrificed to Artemis in order to appease the goddess and thus obtain winds that will blow his naval force over the Aegean to launch the Trojan War. Agamemnon lies to Iphigenia and to her mother, Clytemnestra, to persuade them to join him in Aulis, where the sacrifice will be made. He has moral qualms about the deed, but he does not possess the strength of character to follow through on them and save his child.

Iphigenia in Aulis is not a tragedy about suicide per se, but it does show how a vulnerable young person can be coerced into offering to die "voluntarily" for what are presented to her as noble patriotic reasons. I have friends who have lost children in the armed forces who simply cannot bear the play. I myself was drawn to it immediately because it explores in painful detail how events in families, however rich and apparently successful those families are, can have miserable and indeed fatal repercussions across decades and generations. Through this and other Greek tragedies, I was introduced to the compelling notion of a family curse.[2]

The entire Trojan War and the thousands of fatalities it was believed to have caused would never have happened, Agamemnon tells us in the opening speech, if the wedding of his sister-in-law, Helen of Sparta (Clytemnestra's sister), had been better managed by the woman's father, Tyndareus. He had been so troubled by the fierce rivalry between the suitors for his lovely daughter Helen's hand in marriage that he had made them all swear an oath that if any man should abduct the famous beauty after her marriage, all her former suitors would "marshal weapons, lead an army against him, and raze his city to the ground."

Clytemnestra, naturally appalled when she discovers the plan to sacrifice Iphigenia, reminds Agamemnon of her previous resentments against him. He had killed her first husband and forced her to marry himself. Worse, he had killed her first baby, Tantalus's son, by tearing him from her breast and hurling him to the ground. Not a good foundation for a happy marriage. And she lays out plainly what the consequences of his authorization of the slaughter of Iphigenia will be: how does he think she, the victim's mother, will feel while he is away at Troy when she looks at Iphigenia's empty chair and bedroom? She even utters a disguised threat:

> It would take only a minor excuse
> for me and your remaining daughters
> to receive you home with the kind of reception you deserve.
> By the gods, don't force me
> to become an evildoer toward you, nor do evil yourself.

Clytemnestra, at least, understands that dark deeds have ineluctable consequences for the family.

Iphigenia joins in to trace the chain of tragic events to suffering in another family as well. The Trojan War could have been avoided entirely, she says, if the Trojan king Priam had not exposed his son Paris (Helen's abductor) on the mountainside as a baby, tearing him from the arms of his mother, Hecuba, because Priam had been told that the child was fated to become the cause of Troy's destruction. Paris had survived, adopted by a herdsman, but Iphigenia knows that it was in the countryside where he had been brought up that the three goddesses, Athena, Aphrodite, and Hera, had invited him to make that fateful judgment on their beauty; this judgment led to his momentous choice of Aphrodite, who promised him Helen of Sparta as reward, and consequently to the Trojan War.

This poetic examination of the way brutality within close family relationships creates damage that can never be undone and has ramifications for the future enthralled me. I found it entirely believable that such actions would inevitably turn younger members of the family, who had played no part in those actions, into victims of postponed collateral damage. I was reading the play in my faltering Greek, but I immediately started investigating Greek tragedy more widely, scouring the school library and thrift shops for translations of the other thirty or so surviving plays to read in English. The stories resonated with me to a degree that no others—no fairy tales, television dramas, Disney cartoons, or biblical narratives—had ever done.

I submitted an essay for a prize in a nationwide competition run annually by the Girls Public Day School Trust. The essay was on the Chorus in Greek tragedy, and I still recall my teacher, an austere, impeccably dressed and coiffed, Girton-trained, proudly self-styled spinster, Miss Kathleen Reddish, expressing uncharacteristic enthusiasm as she read out the judges' comments. They had noted the unusually wide range of my reading—covering the entire corpus—for one of my age. I wish I had a copy of that essay. What did my sixteen-year-old self make of the frequently strange utterances and behavior of the Greek tragic Chorus?

My self-education in the extant Greek tragedies, in addition to my set text for the O-level exam, had begun with the *Oresteia*. I had been struck by the darkness in Agamemnon's family. This great tragic trilogy by Aeschylus, the earliest Greek dramatist whose works have survived, was first performed in Athens in 458 BCE. It takes up the story of Agamemnon's blighted family ten years after the sacrifice of Iphigenia, as dramatized in Euripides' play. Agamemnon triumphantly returns to his palace at Argos after the Greeks' victory at Troy. He compounds the shocking injury he had earlier done to Clytemnestra by bringing the Trojan princess Cassandra back as his concubine. But Clytemnestra has already abandoned her husband psychologically. She has been running the city efficiently enough in his absence and started a sexual relationship with his cousin Aegisthus.

In the first play of the trilogy, *Agamemnon*, Clytemnestra murders Agamemnon in his bath; she also murders Cassandra. In the second, *Libation-Bearers*, her adult son Orestes, with the support of his sister Electra and best friend Pylades, murders his mother and Aegisthus to avenge his father. The cycle of crime followed by reprisal is finally broken in the third play, *Eumenides*, in which the newly established homicide court at Athens, the Areopagus, presided over by a misogynist Athena, acquits Orestes. But the celebratory atmosphere at the play's end cannot entirely dispel the sense that the spirits of the dead—especially the dead women, Iphigenia, Cassandra, and Clytemnestra—have not finished casting shadows over future generations of this family.

Aeschylus knew that some families seem to be more unlucky than others, their histories marked by apparently endless feuds and tragic deaths down the centuries. Some historical ancient Greek families, often among the most rich and powerful aristocrats, were regarded as cursed, as they suffered catastrophes across several generations. A notable example was the Athenian Alcmaeonid family, who claimed to be descended from the mythical Alcmaeon.[3]

The curse on this family was thought to have begun in the seventh century BCE. The Aclmaeonid forefather Megacles had authorized the killing of the followers of Cylon of Athens during an attempted coup, even though Cylon had taken refuge as a suppliant at an altar in Athena's temple. Megacles' entire family was exiled for the shocking, sacrilegious murder. Although the dynasty was eventually rehabilitated, during the political wrangles of the fifth century BCE, when the surviving tragedies were composed, enemies constantly paraded the claim that the Alcmaeonids were cursed.[4]

The Alcmaeonids bore much of the brunt of the conflicts surrounding the tyrant Peisistratus and his sons, beginning with their exile by Peisistratus's son Hippias after the murder of his brother Hipparchus in 514. The statesman Pericles, an Alcmaeonid on his mother's side, died of the plague. The statesman and general Alcibiades, another Alcmaeonid, was a highly controversial public figure. He caused the Athenian democracy no end of problems, culminating in his defection to the enemy city-state of Sparta and complicated dealings with the Persian satrap Tissaphernes, whom he persuaded to support the Spartans, before he finally died in ignominious exile. Many Athenians traced the problems faced by the Alcmaeonids and the trouble some of them caused back to the original ancestral crime committed by Megacles. Athenians believed that the gods would eventually make families pay if one of their members committed an atrocity, even if the reprisals took generations to be carried out fully.

Aeschylus presents the form taken by this kind of curse in a number of ways in the *Oresteia,* and in particular the first play, *Agamemnon.* The play, a great poetic symphony on the theme of transgenerational trauma, anticipates some of the ideas we use today in thinking about cause and effect in familial feuds and violence. As a teenager, I found these ideas and images resonating loudly.

Agamemnon centers on three adults whose deaths eventually all operate as sacrifices to appease the Furies (Erinyes), the female divinities who were thought to thirst for the blood of murderers and perpetrators of crimes against kin. The Furies transmit the original damage across generations by driving on other family members to take vengeance. They are closely associated with magic: on one curse tablet a Fury is invoked alongside Hecate, goddess of magic and witchcraft, and on an Attic lekythos (storage jar), a Fury appears in an underworld scene alongside Hecate, a ghost, and dogs. The chthonic, triple-faced Hecate is not the only individual goddess with whom the Furies share features. Their representation as hunters on the scent of their prey brought them into the conceptual sphere inhabited by both Artemis the Huntress and Lyssa, the "dog-faced" goddess of berserk, hypermasculine violence. They were originally envisaged as snakes, and later inherited wings from the idea of the fluttering, feeble ghost of the departed person familiar from Homer. The poet Hesiod describes their origin in his *Theogony:* they sprang, he says, from the bloody droplets which fell on Earth when the Titan Cronos castrated his father, the primordial sky god Ouranos. The Furies are barren, distorted females, born from blood, who destroy rather than nurture. When the haggard, ill-kempt figure Poverty appears onstage in the comedian Aristophanes' *Wealth,* she is described as like "some Erinys from tragic theater; the look in her eyes is crazed and as in a tragedy." In the popular imagination, the Furies become symbols of the tragic genre.[5]

Until they are summoned by a mortal's wrongdoing, the Furies spend their time asleep, often lying on the ground. This may be one reason why they are sometimes said to be daughters of Night or of Darkness rather than of Earth. Their appearance in early classical art can vary strikingly. They are sometimes shown winged and sometimes wingless; they are occasionally black; they may wear long, short, or patterned dresses; they may be topless or wearing cross-bands over their breasts; their hair may be long or short; they are sometimes ugly and sometimes beautiful; some sport snakes on their hairbands, or snakes as hair, or snakes wound round their arms or brandished in their hands; they hold torches, goads, whips, branding irons, even mirrors or scrolls; they may be barefoot or wear elaborate fabric boots. They are often compared with dogs, and their vocalizations with the barking of dogs on the scent of prey.[6]

In *Agamemnon,* the vicious triangle consists of Agamemnon, Clytemnestra, and Aegisthus. None of these characters can eradicate past deeds, and all their actions in the play are the direct result of past actions (especially infanticide) committed by themselves, their parents, or, in Clytemnestra's case, her husband. The atrocious crimes did not begin with the sacrifice of Iphigenia; Agamemnon's father, Atreus, had murdered the children of his brother Thyestes. He then chopped up their corpses, had them cooked in a casserole, and served it to Thyestes, who thus ate the flesh of his own offspring. Aegisthus cannot forgive this atrocity, since the victims were his older brothers. But his uncle Atreus was himself acting in retaliation against Thyestes, who had seduced

Atreus's wife, Aerope. The deaths of both Thyestes' children and the young Iphigenia have left a horrific legacy, and the Furies are thirsting for blood.

Aeschylus chose to set his tragedy about the death of Agamemnon during a single day, a period of hours between dawn and dusk in which the king is murdered. But in the compass of that day Aeschylus conveys to his audience a panoramic transhistorical vision, delving into the past through the successive acts of barbarism among the Atreids, the family descended from Atreus, king of Argos in the Greek Peloponnese. The play also envisions the family's equally miserable future: Cassandra predicts explicitly the deaths of "another woman" and "another man"—that is, Clytemnestra and Aegisthus—which take place in the next tragedy (*Libation-Bearers*). The architecture of *Agamemnon*'s temporal scheme allows Aeschylus to unfold the story of the house of Atreus across three blighted generations. The three central characters have little sense of the large metaphysical and moral wheels in which they are but small cogs. Yet by careful use of the chorus of elderly Argive citizens, the seer Cassandra, and the imagery of human and animal reproduction, Aeschylus allows his audience a much more comprehensive grasp of the endlessly self-replicating violent deaths blighting Argos.[7]

The Atreids' family history contains one instance of a curse being formally pronounced by one individual against another. In *Agamemnon*, Aegisthus reports that when Thyestes realized that Atreus had served his own children to him, "he let forth a great cry, reeled back, vomited forth the slaughtered flesh," and cursed the entire family line of Atreus, including all his descendants, in perpetuity. Thyestes kicked over the banqueting table to emphasize the curse. A sinister detail also appears in the Chorus's memory of the sacrifice of Iphigenia. She is sacrificed to Artemis as if she were a young she-goat, with a bit in her mouth to gag her so as to prevent her uttering her own curse on her father. This expedient does not protect him, however; he is eventually killed to avenge her death.

But Aeschylus presents the curse as taking visual form, as ghosts that haunt the physical fabric of the building. Only the clairvoyant Cassandra can see them, but her clairvoyance allows her to intuit the entire violent history of the palace to which she has been brought. What she has to say to the audience, who know her visions are truthful, whereas the characters in the play do not, is horrific. It so happens that one of my family nicknames has always been "Cassandra," because others have felt that I had a distressing habit of speaking painful truths others would rather deny or at least exclude from comment or discussion.

I have another reason for my identification with Cassandra. I have experienced repeated haunting by both my grandmother and my mother after their deaths, in nightmares as well as in the liminal moments of consciousness that come just after waking, and I find her words menacing but deeply affecting. Cassandra proclaims that she has come to a house loathed by heaven, a house which has witnessed the butchering of family members, the slaughter of men—one whose floor is swimming with blood. Then she points to the roof of the house, at something unseeable by our eyes or those of the Chorus, and screams, "Behold those children bewailing their slaughter and their roasted flesh, eaten by their father." Shortly afterward Cassandra returns once again to the theme of the ghostly children clutching their own entrails and describes in detail the specters of the little boys served up at the Thyestean feast, diminutive ghosts who died in and haunt the house forming the scenic background to the tragedy. "Do you see those young creatures," she demands of the Chorus, "beside the house, like figures in dreams? They are the children, slaughtered by their own kindred; their hands are full of the meat of their own flesh; they are clear to me, holding their vitals and entrails, which their father tasted."

The Chorus cannot see the ghosts, and the men try to understand the nature of the curse in other ways than physical haunting. They see that evil actions are caused in some way by previous bad actions, and adopt metaphors from reproduction. "It is," they assert trenchantly, "the evil deed which thereafter begets more evil deeds, of the same pedigree." In *Agamemnon,* the king's downfall is caused specifically by the working out of the curse, sworn by Thyestes at the infanticidal banquet, against the offspring of Atreus. The Chorus men believe that it is not affluence itself which causes the destruction of a household (a traditional and widespread view) but a single iniquitous deed. The evil deed begets more evil deeds, "of the same pedigree." The criminal act spawns more criminal acts. The Chorus's metaphorical family of parents' crimes and children's crimes then almost imperceptibly mutates into the physical reality of a human family: the doer of the evil deed begets further doers of evil deeds. With another slide between concrete and metaphorical families the doer then becomes the deed again: an act of hubris (insulting, prideful wrongdoing) in the past, the Chorus men continue, "begets" an act of hubris in the present; the "children" of hubris curse the household, but they are in fact replicas of their hubristic parents.

There can be no clearer statement that the miseries of a household are the direct result of former felonies. Bad behavior begets bad behavior, inherited by each child of a cursed family from its cursed parents. While the idea of an inheritable curse may seem superstitious, alien, and primitive to us, it is worth thinking in terms of modern theories about the adverse effects on children of bad parenting or poor parental examples. Dysfunctional families do often produce dysfunctional children, who reproduce, when they become parents themselves, the maladjusted behaviors of their own inadequate parents. This was understood in terms of imitative behavior by some thinkers even in antiquity. Aristotle speaks of a man who was on trial for beating his father. His justification was that his father had beaten his grandfather and he was simply following suit because it "runs in the family."[8]

Seen from this perspective, the archaic concept of the inheritable curse may not seem so bizarre after all. What is extraordinarily striking in *Agamemnon* is that Clytemnestra, the murderous mother from whose body sprang both the victim Iphigenia and the future avenger Orestes, claims that she is the vehicle through which the family curse is working. In her dialogue with the Chorus over the corpses of Agamemnon and Cassandra, she claims that the person the men see before them is not Agamemnon's wife: no, she is an avenger (a fine, strong word in Greek, *alastor*) wreaking revenge upon Atreus by offering up his son Agamemnon as a sacrifice to appease the children of Thyestes. She is the spirit of the very curse, she says, delivered by Thyestes at the fatal banquet. Clytemnestra may enjoy her revenge, but the image implies that she does not feel in full control of what she is doing. She sees herself as a kind of instrument being actively wielded by a far greater force that transcends history and individual grievances.

❖ ❖ ❖

It is now known that there may be a physically inheritable dimension to the specific tendency to suicide. In 2021, the results of the largest genetic study ever undertaken of suicide attempts were published by the International Suicide Genetics Consortium at the Icahn School of Medicine at Mount Sinai Hospital in New York City. By scanning the DNA of more than half a million individuals, a proportion of whom had attempted suicide, the consortium identified a possible DNA feature that increases the risk that the person possessing it will attempt suicide. It consists of DNA variations in a region of the genome on chromosome 7. The results were replicated in a study of more than fourteen thousand veterans. The genetic basis of suicide attempts overlaps with the risk of serious depression, risk-taking behavior, smoking, and insomnia. But the genetic underpinnings of suicide attempts are also partially distinct from those of other psychopathologies. The study provides medical professionals with a new tool to help identify people with suicidal potential, enhance preventative treatment, and lower the risk of suicide, with all its familial and societal implications.[9]

As a teenager, I tried to understand what might have happened in my mother's family line. Perhaps a depressive strand of DNA had been inherited down the generations. Presumably neither my great-grandfather nor my grandmother had been the recipient of a formal curse. But who knows what cruel words might have been said to or by them which helped lead to their suicides and made the consequences of those suicides for others unavoidable? Words said by my grandmother to my mother certainly damaged and wounded her; words said by my mother to me made it difficult for me to feel that I was not somehow implicated in her mother's suicide, despite my being three and a half when it happened.

No ghost has ever been visible to me in my wakeful, conscious state, as the ghosts in *Agamemnon* are to Cassandra. But I have been terrifyingly haunted by my mother and these ancestors in my dreams. I did not live in the buildings in the gloomy southern Scottish towns of Dunbar and Largs where my suicidal ancestors resided when they acted to stop living, but I had spent many weeks in the sunny house in Elie, Fife, where my grandmother had also spent long vacations. I do not think that the Masterton-Henderson family was blighted simply because it was relatively prosperous and outwardly successful: an individual act (whatever caused my great-grandfather's suicide) was instrumental in another individual act of striking similarity.

Finding a way out of the cycle of damage is extremely difficult. A judgment in a court of law that one of the descendants, like Orestes, is actually blameless is insufficient to quell the Furies, the bloodthirsty spirits of the unjustly dead. They were often visualized as ravening dark hounds, each one what Winston Churchill called his "black dog" of despair. But evading the truth and failing to name it can have no effect. It is vital to acknowledge the terrifying black dogs and begin to face them down.[10]

Every year on Mothering Sunday since my mother died in 2016, I have felt a nagging need to send her some flowers. From childhood, I never missed a year throughout the more than five decades we were both on the planet. When in the spring of 2022 the annual wave of despondency hit, even as the gloom of winter receded, I finally felt able to retrieve that ancestral box from the garage.

Leafing through the papers and photographs I began to build up a picture of my grandmother Edith's younger life: her pride in her academic achievements, her delight in her baby girl. I also discovered that my mother had done some substantial research into her own family tree, recorded on an online genealogy tool, and that she had—somewhat surprisingly—given access to it to her son-in-law, my husband, Richard. She had initially disapproved of him as a suitor. He was a divorced father with no particular desire to ingratiate himself with anybody. But he used to help her patiently with computing issues, and she had become very fond of him over the years.

As I emerged from a depression that had set in during the first Covid lockdown and had been exacerbated by problems at work and several sad deaths of people (and pets) I loved, I made a decision: I needed to find out once and for all what had happened in my mother's family line. It was imperative to visit the spots where the suicides had taken place. I wanted to say good-bye to my mother at the place she had been cremated. And it was necessary to do it soon, because the sixtieth anniversary of the moment in 1962 that had informed my whole life was looming. The journey needed to be taken that summer, before October 1, 2022.

My husband and I drew up an itinerary crisscrossing southern Scotland, wrote to local archivists in the different locales to secure appointments, ringfenced a week in July after my academic term had ended, and booked rooms in cheap hotels. Most of this book was written directly after that journey and records what we found, interwoven with insights into suicide and its aftermath derived from ancient Greek texts. Those texts made my woeful private history, stretching back over eleven decades, far easier for me to understand.

Chapter 2

WHO IS DAMAGED BY SUICIDE?

AT THE CLIMAX OF *THE SEVENTH CONTINENT*, A notorious 1989 Austrian film directed by Michael Haneke, the family of three who are about to act on their suicide pact destroy the contents of their apartment. In perhaps the most powerful scene in a continuously distressing film, they smash their ornamental fish tank with an ax, and the fish gasp and thrash as they expire, stranded on the dry surfaces of the living room. They are the direct victims of Georg and Anna's decision to self-destruct along with their young daughter, Eva, who has agreed to die with them; in response to the fishes' suffering, she displays intense grief for the first time in the film. But the streams of water gushing from the shattered tank remind us that others are left behind; we have briefly met Georg's caring parents, and Anna has a depressive brother, seen weeping helplessly earlier in the film, perhaps because their recently deceased mother may have killed herself.[1]

The word *suicide* is not an ancient one. The French claim to have coined the term as a noun in the mid-eighteenth century, but it had already been cited in Samuel Johnson's 1755 *Dictionary of the English Language,* and it has been argued that it was first formulated by Sir Thomas Browne in the mid-seventeenth century. The ancient Greeks used a variety of words with the prefix "self" (*auto-*) followed by a term for killing or violence; the

Romans used circumlocutions such as "fall by one's own hand," or "procure one's own death." But a great many words have been written about what we now call suicide by humans across the planet since the earliest literate civilizations.[2]

In ancient China, the right to kill oneself was denied to children as a violation of their obligation to the parents who had created them. In the Confucian *Classic of Filial Piety,* the imperative of preserving one's own body is central to the fulfillment of one's duty to one's parents. The Hebrew book of Job, on the other hand, features the righteous Jew of Uz at his lowest ebb, deprived of his wealth and children, covered in boils, wishing death upon himself as he addresses what he now perceives as his unjust god:

> When I say, "My bed will comfort me,
> my couch will ease my complaint,"
> then you scare me with dreams
> and terrify me with visions,
> so that I would choose strangling
> and death rather than my bones.
> I loathe my life; I would not live forever.
> Leave me alone, for my days are a breath.
> What is man, that you make so much of him,
> and that you set your heart on him,
> visit him every morning
> and test him every moment?
> How long will you not look away from me,
> nor leave me alone till I swallow my spit?

If only the Lord would turn his gaze elsewhere just long enough for Job to secure his own death! Job's plight is a terrifying challenge to the belief in a providential god, but his story is also educational as a script revealing how *not* to treat someone undergoing a suicidal crisis. Job does still have a wife, but she unhelpfully encourages him to curse God and die. He still has friends, but they conclude that he must have committed some sin to deserve his predicament. Job is understandably not impressed. They are "miserable comforters." We shall see later how Greek tragedy offers far more humane and constructive scripts for dealing with individuals contemplating suicide.[3]

One ancient Egyptian thinker as early as the Twelfth Dynasty of the Middle Kingdom, nearly four thousand years ago, recorded the dialogue a suicidal man conducts with his soul. The speaker wants to cast himself into a fire. He feels isolated and disappointed in humanity. He lacks an "intimate friend." He thinks that death will feel like recovering from a disease, or escaping joyfully from confinement, "like the odour of myrrh, like sitting under an awning on a breezy day." But his soul replies, "Set mourning aside, you who belong to me, my brother! Even if you are offered up on the brazier, still you shall cling to life." The thinking part of the man refuses to accept that he has the right to dispose of his own physical body and predicts that even if he tries to set fire to himself, his instinctive drive to survive will prevent him. But this text, like the majority of reflections on suicide subsequently, focuses exclusively on the psychological experience of the suicidal individual, the ethical evaluation of that person's action, without any consideration of the emotional and social implications for the wider society.[4]

I first felt this lack most keenly when reading Plato's *Phaedo* when I was about twenty. This famous dialogue recounts the events of the day when the Athenian philosopher Socrates embraces his death sentence. Socrates' calm acceptance of his obligation to swallow hemlock after his conviction for impiety and corrupting the youth of Athens has made him a culture hero almost equivalent to Jesus Christ; he is widely perceived as a man who sacrificed himself for a higher cause than his own self-interest—the principle that no society can afford to declare itself immune to moral scrutiny. But it is not often emphasized sufficiently that Socrates had a choice. He was offered the opportunity to propose alternative punishments, and it would have been a standard response in that legal context to ask to be allowed to live in exile. He did not take this opportunity.[5]

After his imprisonment, and shortly before he carries out his death sentence, his wealthy friend Crito, a neighbor from the same district of Athens, offers, as described in Plato's *Crito,* to help Socrates escape. Crito could easily smuggle Socrates to Thessaly, in northern Greece, where he would be financially supported and could live out his days in peace. Socrates refuses on the grounds that he has always been and always will be a citizen of Athens and obedient to its laws. Exile would mean renouncing that citizenship; moreover, he is unafraid of death.

His disciples are distraught. Phaedo, who is from Elis rather than Athens, and is one of those present in the prison at the administration of the hemlock, recalls in the dialogue named for him that while Socrates took his last bath, they waited, "talking with each other and discussing the discourse we had heard, and then speaking of the great calamity that had befallen us, because we thought of him as a father, and that we would live out our lives deprived of him like orphans." Phaedo says that the tears flooded down his cheeks, and he has to hide his face in his cloak, weeping not for Socrates but for himself, because he is losing a friend of such significance. All the disciples break down, but they are rebuked by Socrates, who admonishes, "What sort of behavior is this, you strange men? This was the main reason that I sent the women away, so that they wouldn't hit this off-key note. I've heard that one should die in silence. So keep quiet and endure it." This is callous enough. But it is the two brief descriptions earlier in the dialogue of how Socrates treated "the women" that I was not able to get out of my mind.[6]

In the first, the disciples (not including Plato) arrive at the prison on the day when the death has been scheduled to take place, and find Socrates with his wife, Xanthippe, "holding his little son in her arms and sitting beside him. She cried out, saying to the disciples the sort of thing women do, 'O Socrates, this is now the last time that your followers will speak to you.' And Socrates looked at Crito, saying, 'O Crito, let someone take her home.' And some of Crito's people led her home, howling and beating her breast." But Xanthippe is apparently determined not to be dismissed so lightly by her emotionally constrained husband. After his bath, Phaedo says, "His little children were brought to him— for he had two small ones and one older son—and the women of his household came, and he gave them such instructions as he wanted, and then told the women and the children to leave." Although Socrates spends a considerable time over his bath and good-byes to his family, he does not send Crito back to join the other men so he can say farewell in private.[7]

I was appalled by these two episodes. Socrates was only seventy and had been a powerful and physically fit soldier; he might have had years to live. He had a son whom he had fathered in his late sixties, young enough still to be carried in a parent's arms; he had two other sons of impressionable ages. What went through these boys' minds on this terrible day in the prison, when they were not even allowed to be alone with him as a family? And how did Xanthippe and the other women of the household feel about being sent away to mourn outside when Socrates bestowed on Crito the task of organizing his funeral, normally a duty devolving on intimate kin?

To be fair to Crito, he does seem to think the children merit *his* consideration, for he asks Socrates whether he has any instructions concerning his sons for the disciples to take care of. Even here, Socrates sidesteps his paternal responsibilities, telling the disciples to look after their own souls as a priority, for that way they will serve what he elliptically calls "me and mine." Socrates was not a wealthy man; he even ignored the possible financial plight to which he was abandoning his family.[8]

I am not the only person who finds Socrates' treatment of Xanthippe and his children objectionable. The writer I. F. Stone notes that *Phaedo* "is marred by Socrates' cold and unfeeling attitude towards his devoted wife," which "has too long been passed over in silence by reverent scholars." A neoclassical painter, possibly Franz Caucig, ignored the misogynistic anecdotes about the allegedly "shrewish" Xanthippe that were spread in antiquity and heard her grief instead. The Jewish Austro-Hungarian philosopher Fritz Mauthner, whose skepticism was much admired by the philosopher Ludwig Wittgenstein, wrote a novel titled *Xanthippe* in 1884 (translated into English in 1927) that offers a seriocomic take on Socrates' marriage sympathetic to his wife: Xanthippe is a resourceful woman forced to run her husband's stonemasonry business because he is engaged in cerebral matters.[9]

Mauthner does not evade the ancient tradition that Xanthippe had a bad temper, using the story in Xenophon's *Memorabilia* that her son Lamprocles complained to his father about it. But he makes her irritability more than understandable. We sympathize with her when she urges Socrates to go into exile. She collapses outside the prison after Socrates sends her away and stays there through the remainder of the day he dies. But Mauthner allows her to hear Socrates' last words and portrays her sitting beside his corpse for hours. And he traces her life as a widow, all the way to her death. As the survivor of bereavement by suicide, she has replaced Socrates as the true hero of the story.

And what a different example was set by Socrates' student Aristotle, who died in exile from his chosen homeland of Athens! (He was originally from northern Greece.) Aristotle's denial that the gods interested themselves in human affairs and his scientific approach to the world made him vulnerable to prosecution

Farewell to Socrates by His Wife Xanthippe, 1800–1810,
Fondazione Cassa di Risparmio di Gorizia. (Fondazione Cariplo,
licensed by CC BY-SA.)

on religious grounds. Once his former student Alexander the Great was dead, the Macedonians' enemies in Athens seized their opportunity and charged Aristotle with impiety, the same crime for which Socrates had been prosecuted eight decades previously. But Aristotle did not court execution and martyrdom as Socrates had done.

In his early sixties, Aristotle was suffering from a serious stomach complaint, probably cancer, but he was not a man to give up on life. He took refuge on the estate belonging to his mother's family in Chalcis, on the island of Euboea. His companion Herpyllis, mother of his son Nicomachus, accompanied him. Aristotle died there in 322 BCE. He must have been anxious, and he must desperately have missed the life of the Lyceum (the Athenian institute for advanced study he had founded) and the friendship of his confidant and colleague Theophrastus, whom he had left in charge.

But the move to Chalcis provided Aristotle with a beautiful home, complete with garden and guest house, in which to prepare for the death his medical knowledge as a doctor's son probably led him to expect. He derived emotional sustenance from reading literary works: in one moving fragment, written toward the end of his life, he says that he enjoys the old myths increasingly "the older and more isolated I become." And Chalcis was and still is a healthful, breezy seaside town. It is cheering to think that in his final illness, Aristotle would have taken his last walks along the long sunny promenade, perhaps with Herpyllis and his children, Nicomachus and Pythias, to discuss how best to face the prospect of his death and their future without him. Grief when a much-loved person dies is the worst emotional pain most humans undergo, and it is worth preparing ourselves for it. By choosing exile over execution, Aristotle ensured that his family knew how hard it was for him to leave them.[10]

Unlike Socrates, who casually put the affairs of his sons in the hands of his disciples, Aristotle left behind a carefully deliberated will, as those pursuing happiness for themselves and their loved ones must. Aristotle's will reveals that he has reflected on various potential futures, depending on who among the survivors he loved or felt responsibility for died first. Knowing that he was about to die in circumstances of political tension, and personally facing hostility from some Athenians, he named as chief executor the most powerful man available at the time, his long-standing Macedonian supporter and then governor of Greece, Antipater. Aristotle meant business.[11]

One detail near the beginning of the will suggests that Aristotle wrote or revised the text shortly before he died. His nephew and adopted son Nicanor was to be named the second executor, but he was apparently abroad. Until his return, Aristotle asks that a team of four friends, along with Theophrastus, the (presumably very busy) new head of the Lyceum, "if he is willing and it is possible for him," take responsibility for looking after "the children and Herpyllis and their inheritance." Nicanor is to take special care of Aristotle's daughter, Pythias, "and to see to everything else in a manner worthy both of himself and us." Women without a father were vulnerable to exploitation and needed a well-disposed man to represent them in legal and financial affairs. Aristotle therefore suggests that Nicanor marry Pythias and take over responsibility for her and their future offspring.

Perhaps the most enigmatic figure in Aristotle's personal life was his long-standing lover Herpyllis, a woman from his old home town of Stagira. The reason he did not marry her is probably that she was of lower social status, perhaps a slave or freedwoman. I suspect that he was also concerned for the psychological security of his legitimate daughter Pythias: conflict between stepparents, especially stepmothers, and stepchildren was much feared in the ancient world. The one promise the dying heroine of Euripides' *Alcestis* extracts from her husband is that he will never remarry and thus inflict a possibly hostile stepmother on their children. Pythias may also have been pleased with the instruction in Aristotle's will that her own mother's bones are to be disinterred and buried beside those of her father.

Aristotle also carefully inserted the touching little phrase that Herpyllis "has been good to me." This signals that his executors are to carry out assiduously his detailed and affectionate instructions concerning her: "If she wishes to marry, . . . give her to someone worthy of me. In addition to the other gifts that she has received previously they should give her a talent of silver, from the estate, and three female slaves, if she wishes, and the female slave that she has at present, and the slave Pyrrhaeus. And if she wishes to live in Chalcis, she is to have the guest cottage by the garden. If she wishes to live at Stagira, she is to have my father's house. Whichever of the two she chooses, the executors are to equip it with furniture that seems to them suitable and that Herpyllis approves." Had the mother of Aristotle's son pleaded with him not to let generals and philosophers choose her interior décor?

The provision Aristotle makes for the enslaved people of his estate, though not unheard of for a fourth-century BCE man of property, nonetheless suggests that he had developed warm personal ties with them. They are all to be freed immediately on his death, or at a specified later date (such as his daughter's marriage). Some are to be given generous legacies in addition. Aristotle ensures that not one of the slaves who attended him is to be sold (this would risk their becoming vulnerable to a far less kind master): "The executors are not to sell any of the slaves who looked after me, but to employ them. When they reach the appropriate age, they should set them free as they deserve." The thoughts of such a responsible father, uncle, partner, householder, and friend on any serious matter need to be taken seriously.

I have personally looked at suicide from both sides now. In my youth I knew what it felt like to be in such utter despair that no possibility of a better future seemed possible. The depths of misery that humans can experience are heartbreaking—just being alive and sentient can be excruciating. We must do everything in our power, both individually and as a society, to watch out for signs of suicidal impulses in others and to provide intensive, nonjudgmental support and encouragement. But self-killing inflicts no less damage on others, even if it is qualitatively different, than the murder of another person. Suicide is a death by violence, and like murder it leaves greater scars on the bereaved and on society than a death by natural causes.

What did Aristotle, who refrained from inflicting the terrible legacy of a death by suicide on his loved ones despite his illness and exile, say about self-killing? His argument—the one that has always prevented me from acting on suicidal impulses—lies in a single short passage in his *Nicomachean Ethics*. The passage's prominence seems to indicate that suicide was under discussion in Athens at the time, and that he considered the issue to be in need of clarification. In the passage, Aristotle is considering whether it is possible for a person to commit an injustice against himself:

> The person who kills himself through strong emotion does so against the right principle. The law does not allow it. So the self-killer commits injustice, but against whom? It is apparently against the state rather than against himself. For he suffers voluntarily, and nobody suffers injustice voluntarily. This is the reason why the state exacts a penalty, and there is a certain dishonor done to the person who destroys himself on the ground that he commits an injustice against the state.

That question *Whom does suicide injure?* has been asked far too infrequently by subsequent moral philosophers.[12]

In Aristotle's day, suicide was neither proscribed nor sanctioned by law. Ancient Greeks, at least until the rise of Rome, seem in general to have shared an intuitive sense, however, that it was wrong. An earlier philosopher than Aristotle, Pythagoras, believed suicide to be wrong in all cases; when the Pythagorean Philolaus drew up the laws for a south Italian community, he prohibited suicide. The oath taken by Hippocrates and his medical students promises that the doctor will never give a deadly drug to anyone on request, nor ever suggest that one be administered. An Aristotelian fragment tells us that in the historical city of Thebes, no funeral rites were permitted to the corpses of people who had taken their own lives (although this is not the case in the tragedies set in mythical Thebes, as we shall see).[13]

Aristotle looks at the question from a legal rather than a religious point of view. He asks, Who suffers injustice when a person kills himself? It cannot be the dead person. It must be other people. If you are a member of a state, you do the state an injustice if you make away with yourself. People who kill themselves are held in dishonor. They have damaged the state by destroying one of its members, and this is a form of crime. Aristotle thinks in terms of the wide community, but since he believes that the state is a conglomeration of small communities—that is, families residing in households—he is including the family in the community to which injustice is done.

Elsewhere in *Nicomachean Ethics,* Aristotle implies that some of his contemporaries considered suicide an act of courage, but under most circumstances he disagrees. Killing oneself "to escape from poverty, or sexual pain or sorrow" is accepting death not because one is noble but because one is avoiding a problem. Escape may seem attractive, but embracing it is not brave. And it wrongs others.[14]

People who have chosen not to put their suicidal impulses into action have offered different reasons for deciding against self-killing. But in my case, Aristotle's argument that suicide wrongs others, and so we do not have the right to kill ourselves, sustained my resolve to struggle on in my final year at university. I was young and felt alone, with no dependents or present or former students who looked up to me, so his argument about our obligations to others felt much less compelling than it does now. But it still spoke to me. I wish I could have addressed it to my great-grandfather and my grandmother. They might not have realized how much other people would suffer by their actions. Nobody can predict whose life will be irrevocably marked by another's death, especially a self-willed one. As Sophocles' messenger so insightfully says to the Thebans, "The tragedies that hurt the most are those that the sufferers have chosen for themselves."

What was the "certain dishonor" that Aristotle mentions is done after their deaths to those who have killed themselves? Aristotle does not say, but we know from another source, a speech made by an Athenian politician called Aeschines, a contemporary of his, that when a man killed himself, the hand that did the deed was buried apart from the body. This might be the case only for a death by stabbing or other self-inflicted wound, rather than by drowning or jumping from a height, the methods used, respectively, by my great-grandfather and my grandmother. But perhaps the hand was cut off and buried elsewhere in all cases of suicide as a ritual gesture rather than a response to the precise form of what Aristotle deemed a crime against the community. The removal of the hand does not seem to have prevented the person who died by suicide from being buried alongside his or her relatives in a family tomb, however. The speaker in one of Demosthenes' orations ends his speech by saying that if he loses his case he will kill himself so that he can at least be buried beside his family in the ancestral tomb.[15]

There are indications elsewhere in the Greek world and at different periods that "punishments" were meted out to the corpses of those who died by suicide. Socrates expected to receive a burial appropriate to his station, but the historian Plutarch notes that by his time, early in the Roman imperial period, public officers deposited the bodies of criminals who had been put to death and the garments and nooses (but not apparently the bodies) of those who had hanged themselves in a temple of Artemis at Melite in Athenian territory. An inscription from the third century BCE from Hippocrates' island of Cos prescribes appropriate behavior for a person who comes across the body of someone who has hanged him- or herself: the finder must cut the corpse down, cover it with clothing, then cut down the wood from which the noose was suspended and burn both wood and rope. No priest is to do this; if a priest is the first to come upon the corpses, he or she must delegate the task to another. In some communities, the trees from which people hanged themselves were cast beyond borders or laid at shrines of Hecate set up at triple crossroads far from housing.[16]

When a man hanged himself in the temple of Athena in Lindos, Rhodes, in the fifth century BCE, the goddess appeared to the priest in a dream and told him not to be concerned about her, but to remove the part of the roof above the statue and leave it thus for three days. When the statue had been cleansed by the baths of her father, Zeus (rain), she told him to replace the roof and, having purified the temple with the customary materials, to sacrifice to Zeus in the ancestral fashion.[17]

In the fictional Cretan republic planned by sages in Plato's *Laws* a few decades later, the censorious Athenian seems to classify people who kill themselves out of mere cowardice or laziness, without the justification of an acute or irremediable problem such as public disgrace, alongside kin murderers: killing ourself is as bad as killing a blood relation. The corpses are to be buried in isolated places in barren, unnamed borderlands. They are to receive neither a tombstone nor any inscription of their name.[18]

Christians held similar views about the burials of self-killers: for centuries the corpses of those who died by suicide were desecrated in a variety of ways. As late as 1663 a vicar near Stockholm was suspended for allowing a person who died by suicide to be buried within the churchyard, and it was not until 1823 that the last grave of a self-killer in England was placed at a crossroads, with a stake driven into the corpse's heart and stones placed on his head as a weight to keep his impure spirit from harming the community. I assume that the corpse of neither my great-grandfather nor my grandmother was subjected to such mutilation. But a certain sense of "dishonor" certainly surrounded their last rites. My great-grandfather, Robert Masterton, despite a church service attended by a large and worthy congregation, seems to have been buried secretly. Nobody can say what happened to my grandmother after *her* funeral ceremony. I suspect she was cremated in one of the local crematoriums. There is no memorial stone for either of them.[19]

Aristotle, Plato's student, takes much more seriously than his teacher, or later pre-Christian thinkers from the third century BCE on, the suicidal individual's responsibility to others, and in so doing offers a unique voice in ancient philosophy. Pythagoras, who, as we have seen, also disapproved of suicide, did not use the same argument as Aristotle against it. Pythagoras thought that the injured party was God, rather than the humans left behind. Pythagoras said that no man should depart the station he guards in life until ordered to do so by his commander—that is, by God. But there is a faint echo of Aristotle's position in the phenomenon whereby prominent citizens in Roman imperial times sometimes petitioned the authorities for permission to kill themselves, as the Stoic philosopher Euphrates did the emperor Hadrian around 118 CE. It seems that such a request was informed not only by an ostentatious desire to attract public attention but by a sense of obligation toward the community and perhaps to free close associates from any suspicion of foul play.[20]

But the majority of the influential ancient school to which Euphrates belonged, the Stoics, whose ideas began to crystallize in Athens in the early third century BCE, radically disagreed with Aristotle's position. For individuals who are not flourishing—that is, living life well according to reason and nature—they felt, suicide might not only be justifiable but admirable. The self-interest that makes suicide acceptable, if the preponderance of a person's circumstances are unfavorable, cancels out or trumps any obligation or responsibilities to the community or society at large.

The Stoics distinguished five legitimate reasons for suicide: in obedience to a religious command emanating from an oracle (for example, in order to save one's city); to avoid having to do a shameful deed on the order of a tyrant; when serious illness prevents the soul from using the body as a physical instrument; to escape poverty; or under the influence of dementia.[21]

In the first century CE, the famous Stoic philosopher and former slave Epictetus thought that suicide was justifiable, especially among the elderly, advising his disciples to take as their model the child who quits a game when it no longer gives him pleasure. The Roman philosopher Musonius Rufus used the metaphor of retiring cheerfully from a banquet. Pliny the Elder saw the existence of multifarious toxic plants as an indication that humans are favored by the gods, who have provided means for their voluntary exit from life. He went so far as to declare that being able to kill oneself was the "chief boon" bestowed on humankind; it was an expedient denied even to God, because he is immortal. Pliny the Younger admired the rationality of those who deliberate about whether to take their own lives.[22]

The Epicureans, who advocated a quiet private life rather than involvement in worldly affairs, were less ostentatious about suicide than the Stoics. The Epicurean Philodemus explicitly advocated caution about deciding that the time to die had arrived: a person could never be too sure that the best of life was not yet to come. Epicurus himself argued that life could improve even if a person became blind. The Epicureans also identified some suicides as being inspired—paradoxically—by terror of death: for some, living under the fear of death was worse than a hasty, voluntary exit. But suicide was not discouraged on principle; the Epicureans compared departing life voluntarily with exiting a show at a theater. The Epicurean Lucretius, who reportedly killed himself at the age of forty-four, advocated suicide for those who found life irksome.[23]

But the Romans of all time periods from the early days of the kings before the foundation of the republic in 509 BCE to the collapse of the empire in the fifth century CE generally regarded certain kinds of suicide as noble. They admired women who killed themselves to save what was perceived to be their honor, as in the case of the sexually assaulted Lucretia (even if she abandoned her little children in the process). And Romans tied self-killing to other noble motives. One was patriotism or a patriotic ideal; the numerous suicides of defeated republicans, including Cato of Utica, after their cause was lost to Julius Caesar in 48 BCE were described in Lucan's epic *Pharsalia,* otherwise known as *The Civil War.* The vividness of these passages of poetry earned Lucan the nickname "the Poet of Suicide." Another motive that was applauded was fidelity to conscience (for which both Lucan and Seneca martyred themselves in the first century CE). Even so, ancient Roman sources occasionally suggest that in practice people were aware of the pain that suicide could inflict on family members. The poet Seneca wrote that he thought about killing himself as a young man because he suffered from weakness of the lungs, but the old age of his "very indulgent" father prevented him. Pliny's friend, a jurist named Titius Aristo, was prepared, despite being a Stoic, to endure a long and painful disease for the sake of his wife and daughter. There is an account of the martyrdom in the late second century CE of Agathonice, the devout sister of a Christian deacon from Thyatira, south of Constantinople. The proconsul commanded her to perform pagan sacrifice, while, according to another account, bystanders pleaded with her not to choose death, shouting, "Think of your children," but to no avail. She refused to do the sacrifice, and was either crucified or burnt to death.[24]

It was indeed the early Christians who, inheriting the Jewish proscription of suicide in Genesis 9:5 and Deuteronomy 4:15, took the first emphatically oppositional stance to suicide, creating the stigma and taboos that still linger today. Augustine assumed that the commandment "Thou shalt not kill" proscribed killing oneself as well as others. Lactantius, a North African author who became adviser to Emperor Constantine I when he was first introducing Christian policies in the early fourth century CE, was the first writer in the Christian tradition to declare that suicide was actually *worse* than killing another person. In the thirteenth century,

Aquinas identified three reasons for the Christian ban on suicide and the church's view that the self-killer could never be forgiven: first, suicide did not accord with the natural principle of self-preservation; in addition, it damaged the community to which the individual belonged; and most important, it deprived God of the right to decide when we shall die. The only one of these defenses of the Christian position that resonated with me was the second, most secular one, which Aquinas inherited more or less directly from Aristotle.[25]

During and after the Reformation, Protestants were slightly more sympathetic than Roman Catholics to suicide, some arguing that God in his mercy might conceivably allow forgiveness for self-killing. But the major Protestant thinkers and the subsequent Anglican hierarchy still opposed it virulently. Even John Locke did not include the liberty to kill oneself in his package of natural rights. Yet the arguments challenging the uncompromising Christian position on suicide had begun to appear even during the Renaissance, as ancient pagan authors' views and accounts of self-killing were rediscovered. Although Sir Thomas More did not personally advocate several of the customs practiced by the inhabitants of his fantastic, imagined community in *Utopia* (1516), he did use the literary opportunity to describe a situation in which euthanasia might be permitted for a person who was suffering, or one who was "irksome to others."[26]

In Aquitaine, Montaigne wrote an essay, published in 1580, titled "A Custom of the Island of Cea." He cites numerous classical aphorisms and anecdotes about suicide to support his argument that "the most voluntary death is the finest." He took his title from the ancient anecdote, recorded by Valerius Maximus, a writer in Ovid's circle early in the first century CE, that when Pompey visited the Greek island of Cea (today's Keos), a healthy, sound ninety-year-old woman asked for permission to take poison in front of him. She was leaving behind two daughters and seven grandchildren, and when he agreed, she asked the family to live in harmony, divided up the estate, told her elder daughter to organize her funeral rites, and drank the poison. The Romans, impressed, wept. My emotional response was concern for those abandoned daughters and grandchildren. But Montaigne approved, and he was struck by another anecdote in Valerius Maximus concerning ancient Marseille, a town founded in 600 BCE by the Greeks that was not far from Montaigne's own residence, in which the government officially gave to any citizen who could give the senate an adequate reason for wanting to die access to a public store of hemlock. Montaigne the skeptic took the Christianity out of the equation: suicide became a matter of individual choice.[27]

Defenses of suicide subsequently have fallen into four main categories. The first is theological. The seventeenth-century vicar Robert Burton, who never married and had no children, first published his *Anatomy of Melancholy* in 1638 under the name "Democritus Junior." Burton seems to have imagined himself as continuing in the spirit of the ancient Greek natural scientist Democritus's attempt to identify the physiological seat of melancholy. Burton is presciently interested in the medical dimension of suicide as a symptom of mental illness. But his reason for defending self-killing is theological. It is possible that those who killed themselves did indeed repent of the act before they expired, "betwixt the bridge and the brook, the knife and the throat," so only God can decide the destination of their souls.[28]

The metaphysical poet and dean of Saint Paul's John Donne (who was related on his mother's side to Sir Thomas More) used different theological arguments to justify suicide. He reassessed Christian as well as secular sources to argue that suicide is not inevitably a sin. He filled his treatise on "violent death," *Biathanatos*, first published posthumously in 1648, with what he presents as examples of men from classical antiquity whose suicides are justifiable to escape humiliation, misery, or physical pain, or to save their country: Petronius, a Roman satirist who took his own life after being arrested by Nero; Attilius Regulus, a Roman general said by some to have killed himself when held captive by the Carthaginians; Codrus, an Athenian mythical king who sacrificed himself for his nation in obedience to the Delphic oracle; Herennius Senecio, forced to take his own life for opposing the despotic Emperor Domitian; Hannibal, who took poison to avoid extradition to Rome after the Carthaginians' defeat in the second Punic War; Demosthenes, the Athenian statesman who poisoned himself when being pursued by the victorious Macedonians; Aristarchus of Samos, an astronomer whose suicide is mentioned in passing in a Byzantine encyclopedia; Homer, said by Valerius Maximus to have killed himself out of grief on a desert island when he could not answer a riddle put to him by fish; Othryades, a Spartan general of the sixth century BCE who killed himself out of shame when he was the sole survivor on the Spartan side of a disastrous defeat; Democles, a handsome young Athenian who jumped into a cauldron of boiling water to preserve his chastity when he was pursued by a male sexual predator; Portia, the wife of Caesar's assassin Brutus, who took her own life on hearing that her husband had ended his; Catullus Luctantius, a Roman general who killed himself when condemned to death by his treacherous former ally, Marius; Terence, the republican Roman comic dramatist who drowned himself when he believed that the texts of all his plays had been accidentally destroyed; Zeno of Citium, an early Stoic who held his breath until he died after tripping and breaking his toe; Porcius Latro, an Augustan rhetorician who took his life when suffering from a form of malaria that inflicted bouts of fever daily; Festus, who stabbed himself to escape from an agonizing disease; Bupalus, who killed himself after being mocked by the poet Hipponax; Macer, who chose to end his life to prevent his family being deprived of his property when he was facing a conviction for which that was the punishment; and Charondas, an early Sicilian legislator who stabbed himself because he had entered the public assembly wearing a sword, which was a violation of a law he had introduced himself.[29]

Donne himself felt suicidal at times, especially after the death of one of his children. He had twelve altogether and five of them did not survive childhood. He underwent intense psychological misery and morbid delusions; when his wife suffered a miscarriage, he had a terrifying vision in which he saw her carrying her dead child. He wrote *Biathanatos* around 1607, although it was not published until after his own, natural death in 1631. The Bible, he pointed out, does not condemn suicide explicitly, and Christians tolerate some acts of self-willed death such as martyrdom; why could the tolerance not be extended to other self-willed deaths? To preempt the objection that humans are under an obligation to protect their God-given life and health, he used the argument that Christians do not forbid certain other acts that go against the "natural" imperative for self-preservation, such as ascetic self-deprivation, which deprives the body of sufficient food to maximize well-being.[30]

The second, more influential defense of suicide against the Christian proscription came as an integral component of the Enlightenment. It was spearheaded by the Lowland Scots philosopher David Hume, whose background in Edinburgh and Berwick was similar to that of some of my own ancestors. As a teenager, while reading Cicero and other Roman authors in which Stoic and stoical heroes ended their lives, he had suffered from "distemper," including psychological symptoms akin to what would now be diagnosed as depression. He gave a great deal of thought to the right to die, and worked on his essay "Of Suicide" for a quarter of a century, although it was not published until 1777, after his natural death in 1776.[31]

Hume distrusted superstition, did not believe in an afterlife, practiced an empirical method, and was fascinated by such emotions as sympathy. These characteristics led him to believe that as a society humans irrationally fear bringing about their own deaths even if it would be to their advantage to do so—for example, when they are in pain from an incurable disease. He saw removing the insistence on the sanctity of human life, and thereby removing the taboo from suicide, as restoring humans "to their native liberty"; God has bestowed the power of exercising our will, so he would not object if we exercised it in deciding when to die. Our lives are our own to end as we choose.[32]

Thus far I am provisionally in agreement with Hume. I also agree that there are circumstances, if extreme ones, under which suicide is positively altruistic: he cites the case of the Florentine independence leader Filippo Strozzi, said to have killed himself rather than yield up information to Cosimo de' Medici's torturers. But I become uncomfortable when Hume argues that suicide does not damage society. He points out that some individuals—for example the elderly, infirm, and retired—contribute little to society: moreover, he says, we cannot receive benefits from society when we are dead, so neither do we have obligations.

The problem here is that he argues for the legitimacy of suicide only in the cases of those whose demise and absence would be felt personally by no one. Yet it is not possible to leave life without forcing someone, often a stranger, to deal with the immediate aftermath. Edvard Munch's etching *The Suicide* (1896) conveys this responsibility in the posture of the female pedestrian who has just seen the corpse of a lonely stranger lying on the pavement. A friend of mine was deeply traumatized when a man jumped to his death from a railway bridge in front of her car, even though she had no responsibility for his death. (In enlightened transport systems, railway workers receive special training to help them deal with people killing themselves or attempting to kill themselves on the tracks.) But, even more important, almost every person leaves some family, friends, neighbors, fellow pupils, students, or workmates behind.[33]

David Hume wrote as if suicide were only ever committed by mature, single, childless, isolated men. His admirable mother, Catherine, had raised her three children single-handedly and in straitened circumstances after Hume's father died when he was two. He recalled, "My family was not rich, and being myself a younger brother, my patrimony, according to the mode of my country, was of course very slender. My father, who passed for a man of parts, died when I was an infant, leaving me, with an elder brother and a sister, under the care of our mother, a woman of singular merit, who, though young and handsome, devoted herself entirely to the rearing and education of her children." It is difficult to imagine that had she chosen to escape her predicament by killing herself it would not have damaged anybody.[34]

The most eloquent rebuttal of Hume's position was expressed by his friend Jean-Jacques Rousseau in the epistolary novel *Julie; or, The New Héloïse* (1761). In the novel, the English aristocrat Lord Edward Bomston writes to the young Saint-Preux, whose poverty and lowly status as a tutor have kept him from marrying his beloved Julie and who is considering suicide. Saint-Preux's defense of suicide has been much informed by his classical reading, especially on the subject of Stoicism, but his correspondent is not impressed: "Your death does no one harm? I see! To die at our expense hardly matters to you, you count our mourning for nothing. I am not talking now about the rights of friendship, which you dismiss; are there not yet dearer ones that oblige you to preserve yourself? If there is one person on earth who has loved you enough not to wish to survive you, and whose happiness is incomplete without yours, do you think you owe her nothing?" It is not just friends, family, and lovers who will be damaged, Bomston continues: just because Saint-Preux holds no public office and has no children does not mean that he has no obligation to society:

"You mention the duties of the magistrate and paterfamilias, and because they are not imposed on you, you think you are completely uncommitted. How about society to which you owe your preservation, your talents, your lights; the fatherland to which you belong, the wretched who need you, do you owe them nothing?"[35]

These are powerful words. They have reverberated in my own head on several crucial occasions. Yet Rousseau does not seem wholly convinced by his character's persuasive rhetoric. Although Saint-Preux is dissuaded from suicide, a nonsuicidal death is embraced at the end of the novel by Julie, who has married an older, wise, and kindly man.

Julie has caught a cold after rescuing one of her two offspring from drowning. Most improbably for a mother of young children, she dies happily because she has never recovered from her separation from Saint-Preux, and she hopes that she will one day be reunited with him. Rousseau does not seem interested in the effect of her death on her children or her husband. Romantic love and embracing death are glamorously coupled. It should be noted that Rousseau's many virtues did not include a sense of responsibility toward his dependents. He had five children by his working-class mistress Thérèse Levasseur, a washerwoman, but they were all placed in a foundling hospital.[36]

But Rousseau's atheist coeval and friend Denis Diderot, who neither married nor fathered children, penetrated and exposed the narcissistic vacuity of these male philosophers' inward thinking about the autonomous suicidal agent. In his article on suicide for his famous *Encyclopédie,* a compendium of radical thinking of the French Enlightenment, Diderot argued that suicide violates our social roles and responsibilities to others as well as to ourselves. It affects family, friends, and compatriots. The Enlightenment medic and intellectual Julien Offray de La Mettrie went even farther, claiming that the advocate of the freedom to kill oneself needs to be shown a wife, a weeping mistress, and/

or desolate children, all abandoned on account of "momentary pain."[37]

Yet the voices of these brave Enlightenment atheists, who saw the pain of those left behind as in itself a profound and valid argument against suicide, were drowned out by the late eighteenth-century proto-Romantic glamorization of the doomed lover's suicide, barely circumvented in Rousseau's *Julie*. This was less a philosophical argument than an aesthetic and cultural phenomenon. But it was no less influential for that and therefore provided the third category of suicide justification—an attitude that was in circulation when my great-grandfather was growing up. Novels, poetry, drama, and the visual arts all participated in providing scripts and images of attractive, sensitive young people carrying out their inevitable responses to unhappy love affairs, frustrated artistic creativity, or failure to conform with social conventions and expectations. Goethe's semi-autobiographical novel *The Sorrows of Young Werther,* to which my grandmother gave much attention, was the most significant of these works.

Life began to imitate art, and vice versa. In 1811, the author Heinrich von Kleist and his lover, the intellectual Henriette Vogel, who was terminally ill, carried out their suicide pact. He shot her, and then himself, on the shore of Kleiner Wannsee; their bodies were denied Christian burial and interred where they had died. The site became a tourist attraction. Ten years later, after the painter Constance Mayer cut her throat when her teacher and lover Pierre-Paul Prud'hon married someone else, he could not bear the pain and died, it was said of grief, two years afterward. A celebrated 1830 painting by Achille Deveria shows the impact the discovery of her corpse had on Prud'hon.[38]

The death of the young English poet Thomas Chatterton in 1770, when he was only seventeen years old, leaving behind a loving mother and sister, may have been due to an overdose of arsenic he was taking to treat venereal disease. But an accidental death did not fit with the period's interest in an aesthetically pleasing story about an alienated youth's tragic self-destruction. Chatterton's death was said to be due to self-poisoning: he was an isolated, depressive misfit who failed to make a living wage. Samuel Taylor Coleridge wrote his gloomy "Monody on the Death of Chatterton," making the dead youth into an archetypal image of the tormented Romantic poet; the first version was published in 1790. Alfred de Vigny's drama *Chatterton* (1835) is still performed today; the painter Henry Wallis's *Chatterton,* in which the handsome youth, his complexion deathly white, lies collapsed on a couch beneath a window opening onto a bleak London cityscape, caused a stir when it was first exhibited at the Royal Academy in 1856 and became his most famous painting.[39]

The fourth category of justification of suicide is existentialist: it is usually traced to Nietzsche's proto-existential apprehension of our experiential world as meaningless and without inherent purpose. His concept of the sovereign, autonomous individual, freed from conventional moral values to become a supra-moral being, underlies Zarathustra's speech "On Voluntary Death" in *Thus Spoke Zarathustra* (1883–85). By deciding when and how to die, knowing the best moment to leave, humans assert their freedom and sovereign individuality. But the soothsayer of *Zarathustra* also implies that suicide is a possible nihilist response to the absurd meaninglessness and emptiness of existence, extending the madman's pronouncement that God is dead in the first published part of Nietzsche's *The Gay Science* (1882). Peculiarly, Zarathustra thinks that one of the things that make voluntary death timely is having achieved one's goal in life and produced an heir; no thought is given to how the heir might respond to the action. Nietzsche was himself unable to sustain a relationship with a partner and never became a parent.[40]

"Voluntary death" was Nietzsche's preferred term, in order to avoid the negative and violent connotations of the words for suicide in German. The idea that killing oneself could constitute an affirmation of will and selfhood in the face of an empty and meaningless existence became a staple topic of discussion in existentialist philosophy. Jean-Paul Sartre was likewise struck by the possibility of suicide as an assertion of authentic human choice in the face of alienation, isolation, and absurdity. It is no coincidence that when he turned his hand to adapting Greek tragedy, in *Les Troyennes* (1965), he chose Euripides' *Trojan Women*, at the end of which an utterly distraught, bereaved, and dispossessed Hecuba has to be restrained from hurling herself into the flames destroying Troy. In *Nausea* (1938) the depressed protagonist, Roquentain, recalls, "I felt myself in a solitude so frightful that I contemplated suicide. What held me back was the idea that no one, absolutely no one, would be moved by my death, that I would be even more alone in death than in life." In *Being and Nothingness* (1943), Sartre provides the image of a man poised on the edge of a high clifftop (of course, totally alone), gazing down vertiginously into the abyss but recognizing that he is free—free to live or die a death with certain consequences, making a mark—as he wills.[41]

The suicide note left by Alain Leroy at the climax of Louis Malle's 1963 French New Wave movie *The Fire Within* expresses the Nietzschean-Sartrean view that for people who feel frustrated when their actions do not seem to have any effect suicide can be a means to create undeniable consequences for others. Leroy cannot sustain a relationship with a woman; it is not clear which of the two women with whom he has been involved is addressed in his suicide note, or whether he writes to both, or to the whole world: "I'm killing myself because you didn't love me, because I didn't love you. Because our ties were loose, I'm killing myself to tighten them. I leave you with an indelible stain." Those words— "indelible stain"—sent a chill down my spine as I digested them. Such was the emotional stain left on my grandmother by her father, and on my mother by my grandmother.

To be fair, another prominent philosopher of the time who is sometimes classified as existentialist, Albert Camus, saw the absurdity of existence as something to be positively embraced, and he thus rejected suicide as an option. Life is absurd, but it is in learning to appreciate this that we display our perseverance and humanity. The Greek myth Camus selected to encourage people to carry on living was that of Sisyphus, condemned for eternity in Hades to try to push uphill a boulder that keeps rolling back down again. In *The Myth of Sisyphus* (1942), he concludes, "Sisyphus teaches the higher fidelity that negates the gods and raises rocks. He too concludes that all is well. This universe henceforth without a master seems to him neither sterile nor futile. Each atom of that stone, each mineral flake of that night-filled mountain, in itself forms a world. The struggle itself toward the heights is enough to fill a man's heart. One must imagine Sisyphus happy."[42]

I personally find most constructive the metaphor of life as a waiting room for death, but a place in which we can find ways to make our own happiness and have a great deal of fun. Aristotle's secular ethics can help with this. Perhaps needless to say, I therefore feel far more in tune with Camus's Sisyphus than with the Euripidean-Sartrean Hecuba. And I feel this even though I also agree with Camus's famous first sentence in that book, which asserts that "there is but one truly serious philosophical problem and that is suicide."

So the four main justifications for suicide in favor since the Renaissance situate the defense, respectively, in revisionist theology, individual rights, Romantic aestheticization, and existential despair. None of these arguments provides an adequate refutation of Aristotle's view that suicide injures others. The various discussions are almost always framed, even by philosophers with partners, children, other family, friends, and admirers, as a dialogue between individual male hermits uniquely free of dependents and without the need to be exemplary figures in society; the suicide of, for example, a parent or a schoolteacher is never in the philosophical frame.

A typical example occurs in a letter of the 1890s from William James, widely held to be the founder of psychology, to the philosopher Benjamin Blood (both were husbands and fathers): "I take it that no man is educated who has never dallied with the thought of suicide." But one right can cancel another: even if we have an individual right to kill ourselves, it will almost inevitably violate the rights of those to whom we owe moral duties, as Aristotle, almost alone among ancient and most modern thinkers, intuited.[43]

The modern philosophical position I agree with, and that most nearly approximates to the force of Aristotle's question of who is injured by suicide, is usually called the "role responsibilities" argument, or the "prospective responsibility" argument, which emerged in the field of jurisprudence in the 1960s but which has roots in the Enlightenment position of Diderot and La Mettrie. The role responsibilities argument adopts a broadly utilitarian approach in privileging the welfare of the maximum number of people over the welfare of an individual. Yet it is not clearly identified with any contemporary modern philosopher in particular. The best account is given in Michael Cholbi's *Suicide: The Philosophical Dimensions.* "Each of us has ties to various other people: we are employers or employees, parents or children, members of communities, and so forth. Suicide, on this argument, precludes us from fulfilling the responsibilities associated with these roles. A parent, for example, who takes her own life, fails to fulfil certain moral responsibilities toward her children. . . . The role responsibilities argument thinks of suicide as causing very specific harms to very specific people." Even this lucid exposition, however, does not take full account of the *extra* harm that suicide causes compared with involuntary death. And although I appreciate that the author is, for a commendable reason, consciously alternating feminine and masculine pronouns, the effect of choosing a mother rather than a father as an example of a parent with obligations to children is to perpetuate the philosophers' male-centered tendency to overlook fathers' responsibilities to stay alive.[44]

On top of leaving responsibilities unfulfilled—the outcome also of natural or accidental deaths—suicide inflicts an additional layer of damage because it is still often regarded as shameful. In family conversations it is routinely concealed or evaded, and it makes the work of mourning and acceptance far more difficult. This is why *in practice,* the role responsibilities argument is routinely emphasized by professionals involved in suicide prevention and suicidal attempt intervention. But where conventional philosophy fails us, art and literature may offer insights. Centuries ago, Greek tragedy revealed how suicide exposes the roles and responsibilities left unfulfilled when individuals voluntarily foreshorten their existence.

Chapter 3

VOICES FROM GREEK TRAGEDY: SING THE SONG OF SORROW

"SOONER OR LATER EVERYONE BECOMES A SURVIVOR of someone else's suicide, with various degrees of grief or resentment at the loss," writes Fred Cutter in *Art and the Wish to Die.* Worldwide, more than eight hundred thousand people take their own lives every year, a figure corresponding to one suicide every forty seconds. For the United Kingdom the figure is more than six thousand and for the United States more than forty thousand. Upward of 70 percent more deaths are attributable to suicide than to road accidents. Suicide is the fourteenth leading cause of death in the world. But more than ten additional individuals are closely affected by every one of these deaths, and in some cases the number is far higher. In the previous chapter we saw how little philosophical attention has been paid to the effects of suicide on those left behind, but Aristotle's searching question—whom *does* it damage?—implicitly recognizes that suicide is an event involving a group rather than a lone individual.[1]

Sociologists as well as philosophers have studied suicide in depth, but their work has barely touched on the ramifications for the people left behind by a completed suicide. The sociological view of suicide was founded in 1887 by Émile Durkheim in *Le Suicide.* More interested in causes than effects, Durkheim examined statistical evidence available at the time and distinguished three categories of suicide. Suicides were "egoistic" and undertaken by individuals who were poorly integrated into families and communities, "altruistic" in societies which approved of self-sacrifice in the name of the group, or "anomic" in societies that had broken down, leaving people struggling to survive. He did not ask whether suicide might be imitative or caused by psychiatric illness. Some sociologists also integrated into their analyses Freud's theory of the death drive, or aggression turned inward against the self.[2]

Such views are reminiscent of the ancient intuition that persons who kill themselves might be a danger to others: the aggression can be turned either inward or outward. In Sophocles' *Antigone*, Creon's son Haemon, overwhelmed with anger toward his father, first threatens the old patriarch with his sword before suddenly turning it on himself. The Romans assessed an enslaved man who had attempted suicide at a lower market value, not as a suicide risk, but because such a person might turn this daring aggression against another.[3]

In 1930, another sociologist, Maurice Halbwachs, asserted that the crucial factor common to all suicides was isolation or at least solitude: suicide usually follows an event or circumstance of mind or body which makes the sufferer feel unbearably alone. But four decades later, well after my grandmother killed herself, Jean Baechler published the much more nuanced argument that suicidal motivations cannot be so simplistically categorized; he wrote in *Les Suicides* (1975) that each case is intensely personal and often informed by both genes and psychological experiences. He did acknowledge that certain situations made suicide more likely—above all, a sense of nonintegration, as well as an uncompromising moral code and extended periods of peace. People kill themselves far less frequently during wartime, probably because war reinforces social cohesion and solidarity; more men kill themselves than women because testosterone enhances aggression. But even Baechler overlooks the contribution that the suicide of others can make to the decision to kill oneself.[4]

Among psychologists, rather than philosophers or sociologists, it was only in the late 1960s—too late for my grandmother—that serious attention began to be paid to the people damaged by a suicide rather than to the person who did the deed. In 1964, the obsessively introspective Quentin in Arthur Miller's play *After the Fall* trenchantly explains to his suicidal wife, Maggie, "A suicide kills two people, Maggie. That's what it's for." Four years later, in 1968, the eminent historian Arnold Toynbee described the "two-sidedness of death" as suicide's fundamental feature. "There are two parties to the suffering that death inflicts, and, in the apportionment of this suffering, the survivor . . . takes the brunt." But the key figures in this view were the American psychologists Edwin Shneidman, Norman Farberow, and Robert Litman, who in 1958 together founded the Los Angeles Suicide Prevention Center. The research they conducted there, alongside the practical experience they accrued, resulted in a realization of the profound damage that a suicide, if accomplished, inflicts on the bereaved.[5]

In 1972, Shneidman wrote a foreword to a pioneering volume edited by another member of the center, Albert C. Cain, *Survivors of Suicide,* which contained a series of case studies. The foreword struck a completely fresh note in suicidology because it introduced new terms for discussing survivors of bereavement by suicide. Among psychologists, Shneidman writes, "there is a new sense of suicide as a dyadic event." It has its prehistory, but it also has "sequelae" (sequels, or aftereffects). In a powerful image, he describes how suicide affects the bereaved long term: "The person who committed suicide puts his psychological skeleton in the survivor's emotional closet." Shneidman talks about the "illegacy" of suicide for subsequent generations, and pleads for "*postventive* mental health care for the survivor-victims." He emphasizes that the suicide continues to shape family interrelationships over more than one generation, and laments the absence of "longitudinal" studies of survivors—something that, in a sense, the present book supplies. In particular, he has observed that families often impose narratives on children suggesting that they are "just like" the person who has died by suicide, thus creating a danger of history repeating itself.[6]

It had long been recognized that suicide can have an infectious or "copycat" dimension. In the late eighteenth century a Europe-wide panic arose because young men were emulating the depressed protagonist of Goethe's *Sorrows of Young Werther.* In 1928, more than 150 people drowned themselves in the Budapest stretch of the Danube, mystifying psychologists across the world. Besides the terrible psychological burden that suicide usually inflicts on loved ones and friends, it also sets an example.[7]

Several works from the classical era bear witness to the ancients' acknowledgment of this phenomenon. Plato's *Phaedo* was an instant classic, soon read all over the Greek and Roman worlds, as papyrus finds attest. At least one student of ancient philosophy was inspired to kill himself, even though he faced no problems in his life, after reading it. The poet Callimachus immortalized this man in his "Epitaph for Cleombrotus":

> Having said "Goodbye, Sun," Cleombrotus of Ambracia
> leapt from a high wall down into Hades,
> even though he hadn't been aware of anything deathworthy.
> He'd read the single book by Plato about the soul.

Cleombrotus became celebrated for this impulsive and unnecessary suicide. The sixth-century CE scholar and poet Agathias of Myrine wrote a witty epigram in which a pompous philosophy student suggests that the best way to discover whether the soul is immortal would be to kill oneself. Once dead, being without a body, one would possess only the very soul that one is intellectually investigating and could thus concentrate upon it.[8]

Another philosopher, an Alexandrian named Hegesias, argued with such cogency that death can withdraw us from evil that some of his students killed themselves. He was banned from lecturing on the topic by King Ptolemy II. Some ancient authors recognized a cultural element in such suicides, and Livy, Caesar, and Tacitus remarked on the frequency of suicide among the warriors of Spain, Gaul, Wales, and Germany.[9]

Young unmarried women were believed to be at particular risk of suicide. A treatise attributed to Hippocrates, the father of medicine, on the diseases of young women, attempts to define this risk group. Young women, wrote Hippocrates, when immediately premenstrual, suffer from derangement, mania, fear, and anxiety. They may be delusional and see death as bringing benefits. Hippocrates' cure, which reflects the extreme patriarchal values of his time, was cohabitation and sexual relations with a man.[10]

This medical view of young women's suicidal impulses lies behind the story of the young women of the city of Miletus. In *On the Bravery of Women*, Plutarch reports the "insane impulse" toward hanging themselves that afflicted many of Miletus's young women. Plutarch acknowledged the presence of parents and friends who desperately tried to dissuade the deranged girls, but they "circumvented every strategy and clever tactic of those who watched them," and made away with themselves. The epidemic was stopped only when a law was passed that the corpses of women who hanged themselves would be carried, unclothed, through the marketplace on the route to the grave. The young women were so afraid of this humiliation, even though it would take place after their deaths, that the suicides ceased.[11]

But it was only in the late 1960s that the different categories of suicidal imitation began to be distinguished. Some researchers have examined the upsetting phenomenon of clusters of suicides appearing in educational institutions, where one suicide often seems to spark several others. There has also been research into the contribution to clusters of suicide, or the mass copycat phenomenon, made by journalistic attention paid to the suicides of high-profile figures; Alison Wertheimer, in *A Special Scar: The Experiences of People Bereaved by Suicide* (2014), explores the dangers presented by widespread and sensational media coverage of such deaths. From 1947 to 1968, suicides increased immediately after a suicide story was publicized by newspapers in Britain and the United States. The more publicity devoted to a suicide story, the larger the rise in suicides thereafter. The notion of "suggestion" as a common influence in suicide cases has been scientifically accepted.[12]

The psychologists at the Los Angeles Suicide Prevention Center were more interested in the patterns of suicide afflicting multiple generations of the same family. On the title page of their landmark 1972 volume they quote a medical record from 1901 reporting a remarkable instance of contagion of the suicidal impulse: "A Connecticut man who has just hanged himself was almost the last surviving member of a family that had almost wiped itself out of existence by suicide. At least 21 members of the family had killed themselves over a period of 50 years: his great-grandfather, grandfather, father, brother and 2 sisters. Not all blood relations: one was a woman who had married into the family." It is difficult not to be reminded of the transgenerational curses afflicting the royal houses of Greek tragedy.[13]

More controversial is whether exposure to movies depicting suicide has an instrumental effect in turning people to consider self-killing. Research here is in its infancy, and some psychologists believe that cinema and television dramas that handle suicide sensitively can be useful in suicide prevention and in treating those affected by suicides among their friends and family.[14]

Since the psychologists began to be interested in the "sequels" of suicide as well as the "prequels," cultural representations of the suffering of those left behind have become somewhat more frequent. In the movie *Ordinary People* (1980), the reaction of a character to hearing that a fellow patient in the psychiatric hospital he had been in has killed herself is explored in a sensitive scene with the teen's psychiatrist. Teenage suicide contagion is also examined in *Heathers* (1989). But few artworks of the late twentieth century offer the kind of sophisticated analysis of those left behind by a suicide that is found in Greek literature. One of the saddest poems by Callimachus encapsulates a family tragedy, and the grief of a doubly bereft father and his community, in just six lines:

> At dawn we buried Melanippus, but at sunset
> the maiden Basilo died at her own hand.
> After cremating her brother she could not bear to live.
> The household witnessed the double misfortune
> of their father, Aristippus. All Cyrene went mute with grief
> at the sight of the home of fine children bereft.

Basilo loved her brother too much to stay alive for her father and her compatriots, thus immeasurably compounding their pain.[15]

But the texts in which suicide and its impacts are investigated in most detail are the Greek tragedies. About thirty such plays have survived since their composition two and a half thousand years ago. The tragedies were composed and performed in Athens during the fifth century BCE, when the new democracy was at its height. They were all written and performed by Athenian male citizens and acted before an audience largely consisting of Athenian male citizens, in the theater within the sanctuary of Dionysus on the southwestern slope of the Athenian Acropolis. They all depicted suffering—psychological or physical—and they all investigated the causes of the suffering and its repercussions for the family and wider community. This is one reason why the action of these dramas was generally set at the entrance of a residence, the place where private agony met the public gaze.

The dramas were intended to educate citizens in their thinking about moral and social issues, as well as in dealing with the horrific events and situations that they encountered outside the theater in their personal lives. The plays are remarkable for their nonjudgmental examination of the human condition and the reasons humans struggle. Only some eighty generations separate us from the classical Athenians. Their family structures, along with many of their problems and preoccupations, were strikingly similar to our own, and their tragedies still resonate with modern audiences. This is why Greek tragedy continues to hold an important place in theater repertoires today.

More than two-thirds of the surviving plays feature suicide or self-sacrifice centrally or in a prominent incidental capacity. Almost all the suicides are done by women, but one of the most important self-destroyers is the hyper-male warrior-protagonist of Sophocles' *Ajax* whose death helped me understand my own great-grandfather's. Some suicidal characters leave the stage abruptly and in silence; others reveal their intimate thought processes. But remarkably little moral judgment or criticism of suicide is apparent. Instead, a great amount of sympathy is expressed, both by close family members and by the wider community supporting them. The plays also convey a strong sense that suicide or self-sacrifice can have significant *long-term* deleterious effects on those bereaved by it, especially children. Two plays by Euripides, in particular, directly confront and examine in detail the emotional agonies inflicted by the suicide of a wife and mother, *Hippolytus* and *Suppliant Women.*

I now realize that my repeated study of the suicide scenes in these plays was a way of trying to come to terms with what had happened in my own family, offering me psychological insights that I could not find elsewhere. In 1980 I played the role of Phaedra in Euripides' *Hippolytus,* which was performed as the annual Oxford University Greek play in the gardens of Saint John's College. I learned every word of the play, which had first been performed in 428 BCE, by heart in the ancient Greek. It has sustained me while making me alternately sad and angry throughout my life ever after.

In the key scene Phaedra has gone into the house, telling the chorus of sympathetic local women (played by male actors) that she intends to die but will work out for herself the best way to do so. She had previously made up her mind to kill herself quietly by self-starvation because she cannot bear the pain of her unrequited love for Hippolytus, her husband's son by a previous wife. But now she finds herself in a crisis situation: the information that she is infatuated with her stepson has become public.

The Chorus is shocked, and saddened, and the women imagine her "sinking under her terrible misfortune" while she fixes a noose to the roof beam of her bridal chamber and inserts her white neck into it. Then a terrible cry is heard from backstage, as Phaedra's old nurse, who loves her mistress dearly, calls for someone to bring a sword to cut her down before she dies. It briefly seems as though Phaedra might be saved, but the Chorus is too frightened to enter the house and calls to the nurse, asking her to get slaves to help. We imagine Phaedra physically struggling, breathing her last during this interchange. The nurse is then heard telling someone inside to lay out her corpse. It is too late to save her.

At this moment, Phaedra's husband, Theseus, arrives. He has been away consulting an oracle, and he returns with the conventional garland on his head that marks his sacred mission. The Chorus tells him that his wife is dead, and that she has hanged herself. He is inconsolable, and tears the festive flowers from his head:

Aah! Aah! So why is my head crowned
with these plaited leaves, since my pilgrimage ends in disaster?
Loosen the bolts, servants, that bar the doorway.
Undo the fastenings so that I can see the bitter sight
of my wife. In dying she has killed me too.

The body of his wife is then rolled out of the palace on the wheeled
platform which the ancient theater used to display the results of
private catastrophe to public view.

There follows one of the most affecting interchanges in classical literature. The Chorus and Theseus lament Phaedra with
outpourings of pity and grief, containing only a single brief hint
of condemnation in the Chorus's use of the term "unhallowed" to
describe the death. Euripides alters the medium from speech to
song, accompanied by the double-reeded instrument called the
auloi, which sounded like a pair of small oboes played simultaneously. This shift into melody and lyric happens in Greek tragedy
at moments of heightened emotion. First the Chorus sings,

Alas, alas, you wretched woman, and your sad fate.
You suffered; by what you've done you've destroyed the household.
Alas, you nerved yourself
to die violently by an unhallowed death.
In this wrestling match you are both the thrower and the thrown.
Who was it who cast darkness over your life?

Every phrase, every sentiment, is true to the responses we still feel
to suicide today. The Chorus knows that this act will have great
consequences—it will destroy the household. The women have a
strong sense of the physicality of the suicide—that Phaedra was
involved in combat with herself. The image of the wrestler conveys the horror of thinking about her body twisting as it struggled
against suffocation. The hint of disapproval is far outweighed by

the pity shown to the sufferer, as the Chorus asks who or what was responsible for the darkness that engulfed her. And the women who feel this grief were not even intimate friends of Phaedra's.

Phaedra's husband, Theseus, now picks up the dirge in one of the most exquisite expressions of grief by a survivor of bereavement by suicide in world literature:

> Alas for me and my agony. I've suffered, poor woman,
> the worst I've ever experienced. O Fortune,
> how heavily you've imposed yourself on me and my household.
> An unspeakable stain, but from which avenging spirit?
> This destruction makes my life unlivable.
> Wretched woman, I see an ocean of troubles
> so vast I can't swim to escape it
> nor can I overcome the surge of the catastrophe.
> What words can I use, poor woman,
> to express that heavy burden of what has happened to you?
> You've vanished, slipping from my hands like a bird,
> and have hurled yourself swiftly down to Hades.

Euripides conveys Theseus's shock and pain with pointed images. The king feels her suffocation, as if he were engulfed by a sea of misery from which there is no escape. He struggles to find the words. He senses her absence, and the violence of her departure from the land of the living to that of the dead.

In his next verse, his thoughts turn more to the future after this catastrophic event:

> I want to be beneath the earth, I want to die
> and transfer my home to darkness, wretch that I am,
> robbed of the conversations with you I adored.
> You've destroyed more than just yourself.
> What lethal thing happened to overwhelm your heart?

. . . .

The house is destitute. Our children are motherless.
Alas alas, you've gone, you've gone;
you were the best of women seen by the
sunlight and the stars that shine at night.

Theseus knows that neither he nor their children can ever recover fully from her deed. He feels suicidal himself. He cannot bear the thought of never speaking to her again. The destruction she has wrought on the family outweighs her own destruction. The children have lost a parent. He idealizes her as the very best of women. The loss is inestimable.

It has taken nearly two and a half thousand years for the profundity of Euripides' articulation of Theseus's pain to begin to be equaled in writing about survivors of bereavement by suicide. I have read this sequence over the years again and again. This, or something like it, must have gone through my grandmother's mind when her father took his life; my mother was then deprived of her mother by violent suicide when I was small.

The tragedy, however, does not evade the moral complexity of the situation in which Phaedra destroyed herself. She had become obsessed with her stepson Hippolytus; this is something that may often have happened in ancient Greece, when teenage girls were married to middle-aged men with adult sons by a previous wife. Euripides also suggests that her powerful sex drive has a genetic component: the Chorus recalls the sexual misadventures of her mother, Pasiphaë, who coupled with a bull and gave birth to the Minotaur, and her sister Ariadne, who eloped with her father's enemy Theseus, was abandoned by him, and then became the consort of the wine god Dionysus.

When Phaedra overheard Hippolytus's outraged response to the nurse's proposal that he reciprocate his stepmother's affections, she immediately decided to kill herself. The primary reason was altruistic: she explained before her final exit that she needed to ensure that her own little sons by Theseus were not ostracized on account of their mother's reputation for lewd behavior. In order to ensure their social and economic position, she needed to absolve herself of blame. So she blamed Hippolytus, leaving a suicide note falsely accusing him of sexually assaulting her. In her mind, the choice was between his welfare or that of her own children. When Theseus finds the suicide note, he acts as one overwhelmed with the shock of his wife's suicide might be expected to do: precipitately. He curses Hippolytus, whom he believes to have sexually assaulted Phaedra, though the youth protests his innocence, and as a consequence loses his oldest son as well as his wife. The god Poseidon, Theseus's father, sends a monstrous bull from the sea that causes Hippolytus's chariot to crash, injuring the young man fatally.[16]

Before the action of the play begins, Phaedra had already felt suicidal for weeks because she was infatuated with her stepson. Once that information was leaked by her nurse, earlier in the play, she was exposed to public opprobrium. Phaedra's conundrum—how to ensure that her sons by Theseus are not damaged by public knowledge of her infatuation—can seem absurd to modern sensibilities. It is difficult to imagine that children might prefer to be left both bereaved and psychologically burdened by their mother's suicide than have her with them alive, even if she was known to have made a single mistake when they were young. Nothing can replace her presence for them, and their father is an emotional wreck. The immediate aftermath of Phaedra's death, in Euripides' nonjudgmental poetic hands, offers everyone ever touched by suicide a great deal to think about.

The suicidal woman in Euripides' *Suppliant Women*, probably first performed five years after *Hippolytus*, is named Evadne. This stately, somber tragedy is rarely performed, but it contains an extraordinary portrait of a suicidal crisis and its dismal aftermath. The play dramatizes the extended mass funeral of the "seven against Thebes," the warriors from Argos who fought with the Theban Polynices, son of Oedipus and Jocasta, when he tried to wrest the crown of Thebes from his brother Eteocles. He and several leading Argives died besieging Thebes in the battle which also forms the backdrop to Sophocles' *Antigone*.

Set in Athenian territory at the sacred sanctuary at Eleusis, outside the temple of Demeter, the play opens as a group of black-robed women with shorn gray hair supplicate the Athenian queen mother, Aethra. The Argive king Adrastus lies prostrate at the gate, accompanied by several boys, the sons of the dead warriors. The air is filled with lamentation, but there are no corpses to grieve over. The Thebans refuse to relinquish them. Aethra and her son King Theseus are eventually moved to help the bereaved Argive women recover their dead warriors' bodies according to the ancient religious imperatives of the Greeks.

This results in an armed conflict with the Thebans, in which the Athenians are victorious. The offstage conflict is narrated by a messenger, the attendant of the great Argive warrior Capaneus, one of the deceased. Theseus subsequently arrives with the funeral cortege from Thebes. All the heroes are to be burned on a single pyre, and their bones returned to the next of kin, except for Capaneus. He was struck dead by a thunderbolt from Zeus, which confers on him a special, holy status. He is to be burned separately, his remains receiving interment in an honorific tomb.

As the mothers lament, a crazed young woman suddenly enters in an inappropriately festive costume. It is Capaneus's wife, Evadne. She clambers up the high rocky precipice that lowers over the temple. Evadne remembers her wedding day, exclaiming that she is going out of her mind, like a crazed Bacchante; she has run all the way from Argos to Eleusis (a distance in reality of fifty-three miles!) to share Capaneus's pyre and tomb and "be rid of my life of struggle and of pain." She continues,

I see the termination of my life
where I stand. May fortune assist
my leap. For the sake
of a good reputation
I'll hurl myself from this rock,
leaping into the fire,
mingling my remains
with my husband's in the gleaming flames,
lovers' flesh in close contact.
I shall enter the halls of Persephone.

Evadne recognizes that she is out of her mind, like a crazed follower of Dionysus, and yet she has a clear and precise understanding of her physical position high on that rock. She anticipates the jump she plans to make, and the sensation of quasi-sexual physical contact her body will have as it burns with her husband's.

But before she throws herself from the rock, a terrible dialogue is conducted in the last moments of her suicidal crisis. Her elderly father, Iphis, appears. He has followed her from Argos. He is already bereaved, since one of the dead warriors was his son (Evadne's brother), Eteoclus. In an interesting detail, he says that Evadne had formerly been under careful supervision, with guards on the door, because of her "desire to die with her husband." This implies that it was known she was psychologically disturbed to a potentially suicidal extent from the moment Capaneus set out on campaign.

The reason she was recently left unsupervised was, Iphis explains, his own current problems and preoccupations. He had neglected his daughter in her state of psychological breakdown. He is, however, convinced that he will find her at Eleusis, and he asks the Chorus if anyone has seen her. This whole passage is fascinating; it shows that Euripides' audience knew that women could become deranged with anxiety when their menfolk were away at war, that suicidal people need to have a watch kept over them, and that a parent might have an accurate insight into a particular child's distinctive psychological makeup.

Evadne sees her father, and shouts at him, "Here I am, on the rock in my misery, hovering lightly over Capaneus's pyre like some bird!" In common with many who wish to kill themselves, she has escaped supervision by trickery, for fear, she says, that her family will be angry with her. And then her delusional state becomes apparent as she describes her goal: it is to win a "prize of victory" over every other woman, a prize for her courage in her loyalty to her husband. Iphis is embarrassed as well as shocked and pleads with her not "to talk like that before the masses." In her narcissistic fantasy, Evadne claims that publicity is exactly what she wants. Iphis summons his inner patriarch and forbids her to leap. In response, she delivers her last words as she takes the jump: "It doesn't matter. You will never get hold of me. Look, I throw myself down, bringing no joy to you, but instead to myself and my husband, blazing on the pyre."

Evadne's shocking leap to her death, acknowledging that she is serving her own emotional interests at the expense of her father's, not only demonstrates that war ruins lives but, in an inspired piece of writing, makes Evadne herself echo the competitive, masculine ethos which started the war in the first place. Like a Homeric hero, she has come to win eternal renown by dying gloriously. In Thucydides' *History of the Peloponnesian War,* Pericles tells the bereaved women of Athens that they must not lament noisily in public; their greatest glory will be to be spoken of as little as possible, whether in praise or blame. He would not have approved of Evadne, who ensures that the grief of her widowhood is remembered for all time, nor of the chorus of Argive mothers, who lament insatiably.[17]

In her last speech, Evadne seems to *revel* in the pain she is inflicting on her father. She never even mentions her little son,

Edward Francis Burney, *Evadne Throws Herself on the Funeral Pile of Her Husband Capaneus*, 1790–1800. (The Metropolitan Museum of Art, Gift of Spencer Bickerton, 1933; metmuseum.org.)

Sthenelus, who must have been among the boys present and would have witnessed his mother's horrific demise. The Chorus is reminded of the agonies and suicides undergone by Oedipus and his family across the generations, agonies which caused the very war in which Capaneus died. And the play ends with the women performing an antiphonal lament with the little boys, including Sthenelus, who carry the urns containing their fathers' bones from the pyres.

Iphis delivers an excruciating speech about his plight, as a man bereft of his son by combat and his daughter by suicide. He is given far more attention in the play than the young woman, whose suicidal crisis scene is as short as it is unexpected. Iphis wishes he could live his life over again, using his new knowledge to forestall his children's deaths. He asks what possible option is open to him now:

So what should I do in my wretchedness?
Should I go home? That way I would see the desolation of my house,
with its many rooms, and my life's futility.
Or should I go to the home of Capaneus here,

which used to give me the greatest delight when this daughter of mine
    was there?
But she is no longer alive, the woman who would pull my
cheek down to her lips, and take my head in her hands.
There's nothing sweeter to an aging father than a daughter.
The male children have stronger souls,
but their caresses are less delightful.

He cannot even bear to attend his daughter's funeral:

O! take me to my house at once, hide me in darkness, to waste and
fret this aged frame with fasting! What shall it benefit me to touch
my daughter's bones?

He declares his intention of starving himself to death. There is
to be another suicide in the household of Iphis, and he seems as
little concerned for the effect it will have on Evadne's offspring
as she had been.

Victorian classical scholars were appalled by Evadne's suicide.
It did not simply contravene the broad ancient Greek convention, of which these emotionally restrained scholars approved, in
which violent death was not represented visibly onstage. Worse,
they noticed its parallels with the Rajput practice of *sati* (*suttee*),
by which (mostly elite) Hindu widows immolated themselves
on their husbands' pyres. The hideous custom had horrified
British gentlemen of the Raj, who tried to stamp it out (often
by taking equally horrendous measures). The idea that the revered
and exemplary ancient Greeks might have engaged in such
a ritual was felt to be so shocking that Evadne's scene was
frequently denounced as an interpolation and excised from the
text. It was argued that Greeks would never have heard of self-
immolation by widows before Alexander the Great reached India a
century later.

But such an argument overlooked both the regularity with which women whose husbands or lovers have died turn in ancient storytelling to suicide and Euripides' interest in psychology. In his plays he portrays several different manifestations of psychological disturbance. The ancient Greeks distinguished mental illnesses by associating their causes and symptoms with discrete gods. Such forms of insanity ranged from Phaedra's lovelorn self-starvation before she takes more decisive suicidal action, both caused by Aphrodite, to Cassandra's prophetic frenzy when she is possessed by Apollo in *Trojan Women*. Orestes' obsessive need for revenge and attendant psychotic episodes in several plays, including Euripides' *Electra* and *Iphigenia Among the Taurians* and Aeschylus's *Orestes,* are inspired by the barking female Furies. Heracles' psychotic delusion, in which he kills his wife and children, in Euripides' *Heracles Mad* is caused by the goddess of berserk warriors, Lyssa; Queen Agave has been made to hallucinate in a mania caused by the wine god Dionysus when she hunts down her son Pentheus in Euripides' *Bacchae.* But Evadne, although clearly disturbed, is neither possessed by a deity nor, strictly speaking, delusional. She may represent a known phenomenon among the war widows of ancient Greece. It is highly unlikely that no woman had ever killed herself when receiving news that her husband had been killed in combat, and Euripides explores how such a response might play out in a moment of extreme social tension.

These dramatic accounts of suicide and its consequences are prescient, rare, and valuable. It was only in the very late twentieth century that the experiences of those left behind once again came under serious scrutiny in literature. Before this explorations of such feelings were "virtually unheard of . . . and perhaps hardly conceivable in an age when suicide or self-slaughter was so categorically othered."[18]

Although suicide has always been central to specifically tragic theater, including that of Shakespeare and the Jacobeans, it is hard to find any dramatists who focus on its impact on the bereaved until recently. The American playwright Marsha Norman's *'night, Mother* (1981) did portray a mother's deep shock as her daughter prepares to kill herself, but it ends with the death rather than its long-term impact. *Every Brilliant Thing,* a play by Duncan Macmillan (2013), however, places center stage the response of a small boy to the suicide attempt of his mother in an astute, tender, and often comical way. Alice Birch's *Anatomy of a Suicide* shocked audiences at the Royal Court Theatre in London in 2017 by its premise that suicidal depression plays itself out transgenerationally, afflicting a mother, her daughter, and her granddaughter. Their stories are enacted simultaneously in a bravura exercise in scriptwriting. But it is in the medium of the memoir that most progress has been made in giving truthful voice to the experience of those bereaved by suicide.

The reactions to the death of the novelist David Foster Wallace were a breakthrough. His friend Jonathan Franzen published an essay in the *New Yorker* in 2011 in which he recalls visiting Wallace's widow, Karen Green. She asked him to scatter some of Wallace's ashes on an uninhabited volcanic island he was about to visit. Franzen thinks about the "emotional violence" involved in the staging of the death scene, since Wallace hanged himself on his patio to be discovered by his wife. Franzen writes, "To deserve the death sentence he'd passed on himself, the execution of the sentence had to be deeply injurious to someone. To prove once and for all that he truly didn't deserve to be loved, it was necessary to betray as hideously as possible those who loved him best." Green, an artist, said in an interview the same year that when the person one loves kills himself time stops. "Life becomes another code, a language that you don't understand."[19]

She subsequently published an extraordinary memoir-artbook, *Bough Down* (2013), in which she describes dreaming about someone being punished for putting himself to death. For a long time she was unable to be creative at all. But eventually, art helped her begin to find a way through her pain; her path involved not only addressing her own agony but actively reconstructing in her mind, and confronting head-on, the despair her husband had suffered. This is what I try to do in the following chapters, in which I excavate the buried pain of my great-grandfather and my grandmother, and supplement their tales with insights from the Greek tragedies I have been reading and finding comfort in for most of my life.[20]

Chapter 4

THE GREAT-GRANDFATHER'S TALE

MY GREAT-GRANDFATHER ROBERT MASTERTON, A proud, fractious, and intractable man and a distinguished member of his community, ended his life in the summer of 1912 beside the sea on the south bank of the Firth of Forth. Ajax, an equally proud, quarrelsome, and stubborn individual, the greatest Greek warrior at Troy after Achilles, ended his life in the late Bronze Age on a beach in northwestern Anatolia not far from Troy. Sophocles' *Ajax* depicts the horror of this tragic suicide and its impact on the hero's family and community. Scholars and theater professionals have recently cited this emotionally rich text as evidence that posttraumatic stress disorder was prevalent among the military in antiquity, but the play's most profound psychological truth lies in its detailed analysis of a suicidal crisis undergone by a proud, successful, taciturn, and irascible man who feels humiliated and cannot ask for help.[1]

Ajax comes from a small island kingdom and is not among the wealthiest warriors at Troy. He has been slighted by his army and then made to look ridiculous by his own bizarre conduct during a psychotic episode inflicted on him by Athena after he expressed insufficient gratitude to the gods. He kills himself a little over halfway through the play. The first half traces his psychological journey through delusional behavior, public humiliation, despair, and pressure from his dependents not to give up, to deceit, as he evades their supervision, and finally to angry, violent self-killing in total isolation. The remainder of the play portrays the grief of his family and a terrible quarrel among the authority figures over what should be done with his corpse. Eventually they agree that he should be allowed a decent burial.

Ajax's story contains several parallels with my great-grandfather's, and my own thinking about the repercussions of the bleak events of that August week in 1912 was suddenly illuminated as an undergraduate at Oxford when I was involved in a performance of Sophocles' *Ajax,* playing the part of Athena. My elder brother, who was then a postgraduate student, took the role of Ajax himself, thus bringing home to me even more pointedly the relevance of Ajax's tragedy to our family history.

The play opens with Athena telling Odysseus that Ajax is in a state of delusion. He was outraged when the Greeks had awarded the arms of the deceased Achilles not to him, the most brilliant surviving Greek warrior at Troy, but to the crafty Odysseus. Ajax has been sent mad by Athena, who diverts his intended slaughter from his great enemies, the sons of Atreus (Agamemnon and Menelaus), to the Greeks' livestock and the men set to guard the animals. He has now rounded up some of the remaining cows and sheep, and is goading and taunting them in his tent. Athena summons the deluded hero outside and enjoys mocking him in front of the appalled Odysseus.

The Chorus consists of Ajax's own regiment, men like him from the island of Salamis, who feel helpless now that their great leader has incurred such public shame. They know he has enemies and fear "the clamor of their evil tongues." The Chorus desperately tries to understand what force or god can have afflicted Ajax with madness, and why.

Ajax then comes to his senses, and is horrified to discover what he has done. He makes it clear that he is suicidal, begging his men to kill him, and beseeching the lord of the underworld to take him immediately. He juxtaposes the prowess of his father, Telamon, as a warrior with his own disgrace, and states baldly that he cannot return home to face the grand old man. He considers attacking the Trojans single-handedly in order to meet a speedy death in combat, but he does not want to help his own side because the Greeks have dishonored him. So he decides to kill himself: "The options for a noble man are only two: either live with honor, or make a quick and honorable death." This could scarcely be more explicit.

The pain of those who fear bereavement by suicide is expressed with memorable cogency by Ajax's concubine, an enslaved woman he captured during the war, named Tecmessa. Her position, should he die, would be extremely vulnerable, but she is also concerned about the cruel things that will be said about her if he takes his own life, for suicide brings a special opprobrium. Her more immediate concern is that she will be violently appropriated as a sexual partner by another Greek warrior and that the little son, Eurysaces, she bore Ajax will be enslaved. These actions will compound the mother and son's private sorrow with a terrible loss in power and status. Tecmessa remarks that Ajax's suicide would also dishonor his father and mother and leave them desolate; Ajax's mother is still relatively young and misses her son intensely.

Tecmessa ends her remarkable speech with a psychologically sophisticated appeal. She asks Ajax to think about his relationship with her:

> A man ought to cherish memories,
> if he has experienced anything pleasant.
> Kindness always produces further kindness.
> Where a man erases his memories of being treated well,
> then he stops being a noble one.

Tecmessa has been good to Ajax, and she deserves his consideration. He has a reciprocal obligation to her. She seems to envisage the possibility of their living together back in his parental home in Salamis, despite the humiliation that has befallen him at Troy. She also redefines "nobility" of character. Nobility is not the prideful escape from pain he is contemplating; it is looking after those who have looked after him. These words remind me forcibly of Aristotle's decisions to stay alive after Athens rejected him and to look after the interests of Herpyllis, the mother of his son, because she "has been good" to him.

Ajax, however, is unmoved. His attitude becomes even more frightening as his little son is brought to him. Ajax believes that although Eurysaces is young enough to be carried in his mother's arms, he will surely not be alarmed by seeing his father covered in gore—at least, not if he has inherited a properly manly spirit: "He must be broken in like a colt into his father's brutal ways and not fail to equal him in nature." Ajax now makes the poor child wield his massive shield, made of seven layers of oxhide. These shields were so heavy that they challenged a grown man to support them in the battle line. Ajax also says farewell to the Chorus men, his regiment, before harshly ordering Tecmessa to take the boy inside,

> and don't make noisy laments
> outside the tent. What a terribly weepy thing is a woman!
> Quick, close the doors. A skillful doctor doesn't
> utter spells and dirges when a wound needs the knife.

Ajax's emotional callousness toward his tearful mistress is breathtaking. Nor is there much ambiguity about his phrase "when a wound needs the knife." When she pleads with him further, he rebukes her. Together with the child, the couple enters the tent.

Some minutes pass while the Chorus, left alone, muses on Ajax's strange state of mind, how he "is grazing his thoughts in isolation, becoming a great source of sorrow for his friends." The soldiers picture his mother, cast into grief on hearing the news that her son has a "disease that destroys the mind." They even wonder whether this sick man, whose "mind wanders outside itself," might, given his continuing derangement, indeed be better off in Hades.

Ajax wants to kill himself, but he needs to escape the supervision of the mother of his child and that of his men, who will surely try physically to restrain him if he makes an attempt on his life. Like many men intent on suicide, he employs deception. When he emerges from the tent with Tecmessa, he delivers a rhetorically polished speech in which he pretends that he has changed his mind and has decided to serve the Atridae once more as an obedient warrior. He even claims that he feels pity for Tecmessa and Eurysaces. He sends both Tecmessa and the Chorus away after convincing them that he is not a suicide risk any more.

It is most unusual for a Chorus to leave the stage during a Greek tragedy; that it does so here suggests that Sophocles wishes to emphasize the distinctiveness of Ajax's behavior. And now, a little over halfway through the play, Ajax delivers his last words, alone near the seashore (like Robert Masterton). He then plants his sword in the ground and falls upon it. As noted earlier, violent death hardly ever occurs onstage in Greek tragedy. Ajax's titanic temperament causes Sophocles to break even this fundamental convention of the genre.

My great-grandfather's death was not mythical but historical, and it flouted social conventions and outraged Christian proprieties rather than breaking the rules of a literary genre. Robert Masterton was a tall, saturnine, solidly built middle-aged man, who was found drowned in Dunbar's Seafield Pond, then known locally as the Old Brickworks. His body was seen floating by a man who lived nearby; it was brought to shore, but all attempts to revive him failed. The article reporting the death and funeral in the *Haddingtonshire Courier* of August 16, 1912, reveals that his community was shocked by the suddenness of this gloomy discovery. Masterton had been seen in town and at his office during the afternoon, "and consequently the news of his demise came as a great surprise to his relatives and friends." The article never uses the word *suicide,* nor even any euphemistic paraphrase. But the appalled tone is unmistakable.[2]

The funeral took place speedily, three days later, on Thursday, August 15. It was conducted "from the parish church"—a severe mock-Gothic edifice built in 1821 that perches on a small hill to the south of the town center—with the sound of seagulls crying overhead. There is no indication of what that *from* in the newspaper article signifies. This is how the newspaper describes the public part of the ceremonies:

> A very large and representative congregation was present, including the Provost [whose name was John Low], Magistrates, and Town Council, and the Parish Council. The service was conducted by Rev. Wm. Borland, minister of the parish, and Rev. Melville Stewart, Belhaven Church. The funeral was attended by some hundreds of the citizens, and at the interment a very large concourse of the general public were present. Mr Hugh K. Cooper presided at the organ, and played the "Dead March" from Handel's "Saul" as the coffin was carried from the church. Numerous places of business in the burgh had their blinds drawn, and the Parish Church bells tolled while the remains were being carried to their last resting-place.

When I re-create this scene in my mind, I can hear the famous work by Handel resounding in my ears. It is the most celebrated part of Handel's oratorio based on 1 Samuel, first performed at the King's Theatre, London, in 1739, and a staple of choral societies across Britain.

The funeral anthem for Saul, his son Jonathan, and the other Israelite dead is played in act 3 of the oratorio, after they die in battle with the Amalekites, thus preparing the way for David to inherit the Kingdom of Israel. The magnificent music requires an organ (Handel himself played this instrument in early performances), trombones, woodwinds, and timpani. Unusually for a funeral march, it is in a major key, C, which lends dignity and magnificence, as well as a faint note of optimism that nonetheless does nothing to diminish its plangent mournfulness and solemnity. The imposing piece of music became an instant classic, performed at numerous state funerals, including those of George Washington, Lord Nelson, and the duke of Wellington. It was played in 1909 at the funeral of Robert Masterton's locally eminent father-in-law, John Kellie Keir. It was a mark of the greatest respect to Robert Masterton that it accompanied his cortege on that late summer day in 1912. He had taken his own life, but his corpse was deemed worthy of the music chosen to honor the greatest men in the nation.

The sermon preached in the parish church by the Reverend William Borland on the Sunday following the suicide and the funeral expressed the difficulty the local people were having in processing the manner of Robert's death: "We try to understand that meaningless end to a life which was so vigorous and so useful. ... What is the meaning and the purpose of this dark mystery of providence and personality?" Borland also felt the need to defend Robert's reputation from harsh criticism of his decision to kill himself, perhaps from those whose piety was most traditional and conservative: "Let us be silent. ... Let us be humble; we have great need to be, and let us refrain from judgement—lest we be judged."[3]

Robert Masterton's self-drowning created such a scandal because he was a prominent member of the local community, successful in public life and the church. The minister reminded the

John Kellie Keir, Provost of Dunbar, 1896–99 and 1899–1909.
(Author's collection.)

congregation of "his indefatigable, his invaluable public services."
He had a wife and four healthy children who had survived into
young adulthood; he had fairly recently bought a splendid villa in
the center of the town to house them. Why did he so suddenly take
his own life? We can never be certain of the motivation of those
who have killed themselves, but the second part of the newspaper
article offers a few hints.

Before moving on to these, it is worth asking what life was like
in the Mastertons' household. My mother once said that Robert's
wife, Mary (née Keir), was "difficult," but she had never personally
met her grandmother, who died before she was born. The idea
that she was difficult must have come via my grandmother Edith;
but many daughters, especially those who dote on their fathers,
find their mothers difficult. Mary had also endured great sadness
when two of her three younger brothers died young; Alfie when he
was eighteen at the family home on December 3, 1885, a year after
her marriage; and Peter in 1900 at the age of twenty-eight. In the
eight years preceding her husband's suicide she had also lost her
mother, uncle, and father in swift succession. She may well have
been hard to live with at times.

Perhaps Robert found all his in-laws difficult. By marrying
Mary Keir, he had leapt up the ladder of the Scottish class system, bypassing several rungs. Her father, John Kellie Keir, like her
uncle, John's older brother Peter, was the son of a successful and
prosperous boatbuilder at a time when every industry in eastern
Scotland depended on maritime trade and transport. John and
Peter followed their father in the same line of business and made
good money; they had their own two boats, *Bass* and *May*, named
after the landmark islands visible from both sides of the Firth of
Forth. John was elected to the Dunbar council in 1874 and soon
became a bailie (magistrate), and then first bailie. In 1896 he was
provost (mayor), and in 1897 played a leading role, with his wife,
in the Jubilee celebrations. In 1899 he returned to the magistracy

Dunbar Parish Church. (Photograph by Richard Poynder, reproduced by permission.)

until his death in 1909. His brother Peter took a similar career path in the larger East Lothian town of Musselburgh, where he served as provost at the same time John was mayor of Dunbar.

Robert, a newcomer from Newburgh in Fife, was essentially marrying into one of the most important and visible families on the southern bank of the Firth of Forth, and the Keirs may have made him very aware of their difference in status. The three Dunbar houses he lived in with Mary and their children increased each time they moved in size and grandeur, perhaps implying a desire to impress his successful father-in-law. Yet Robert may have had financial worries—a common motive for male householders to contemplate suicide ever since it was presented onstage by Aristophanes' demotic Athenian protagonists Strepsiades in *Clouds* and Philocleon in *Wasps*.

Robert had been born into a far humbler, working-class family. His father, James Masterton, had originally been a merchant seaman, but in the 1851 census was identified as a textile worker, a "warper" of linen threads. James's wife, Mary (née Spence), almost certainly did the same work, but for lower wages. The two prepared threads for the factory weaving machine by laying them out in lines on a large cylinder called a beam. The factory at which they worked and where they were housed was at the back of a shop on Newburgh High Street in northern Fife. The industry was failing by the time Robert was born. The factory owner, James Lyell, declared bankruptcy in 1849 but continued to run the factory for several more years. His employees often had to turn their hands to seafaring as merchant crew or fishermen when business was bad. The linen industry had been transformed with the introduction of the power loom, which arrived in Scotland in 1821. But it is likely that Robert and his siblings were made to work in the Newburgh factory alongside their parents. They probably escaped hard labor until they were nine under the terms of the Factory Act of 1833, which had also somewhat limited the total weekly hours a child between nine and thirteen years of age could be made to work. (Before that landmark legislation, nearly half of all working children were dead before they reached the age of ten.)[4]

Newburgh linen was world famous, but the labor involved in transforming flax into fabric was immense. Flax had been introduced into Scotland by the Romans, and it was grown across the eastern Lowlands. The Newburgh linen manufacturers sent their employees by steamboat across the Tay to purchase bundles of prespun flax in Dundee. It had to be washed before it could be woven, and dried in and around the factory premises, hanging from poles. In wet weather this made domestic life most uncomfortable and the air unhealthily damp. A local historian in 1871 lamented the rates of premature death in the burgh, which were far higher than the national average, resulting from widespread alcoholism, insanitary housing conditions, persistent shortage of clean water, and typhus.[5]

Robert was the youngest of twelve children born to his father and mother, but one brother had died before he was born, and at least three other siblings—two brothers and a sister—died during his childhood while they were all living in the factory housing. His mother died when he was only twenty. She had been a great beauty, and a surprising piece of evidence suggests that she lived in far greater poverty with her husband than she had been accustomed to in childhood: a pencil drawing of her as a very young woman survives by Erskine Nicol, a Scottish artist of some reputation. But she had lived her married life under humble circumstances at the linen factory, where she had produced twelve children in less than twenty years, and lost several of them. There is no record of her death, but I have sometimes wondered whether this presumably exhausted wife and mother considered or even succeeded in taking her own life.

At twenty-one, in June 1876, the now motherless Robert sailed from Glasgow on the *State of Nevada,* a State Line Steamship Company vessel built on the Clyde, and entered the United States at New York. He seems to have been a crew member, so he apparently followed his father's earlier profession of merchant seaman, though his choice to work on the cross-Atlantic line may imply that, like so many impoverished young Scotsmen at the time, he was considering emigration. But he must have returned to his home country soon afterward, since his next recorded appearance is in Glasgow a couple of years later.

Coming from a background of poverty and deprivation, Robert brought personal experience to the line of work he then entered. He worked in Glasgow as inspector of the poor, employed by the Govan Parochial Offices to report on the desperately impoverished dockyard workers and shipbuilders of that rough district on the Upper Clyde. He lived for a while in the notoriously squalid tenement area known as the Gorbals. Yet he married the well-

Erskine Nicol, Pencil portrait of Mary Masterton. (Author's collection.)

born Mary Keir on November 27, 1884, and the celebration was held at her parents' lovely home, Woodbush Cottage, in Dunbar, which was and remains today a substantial six-bedroom mansion with gardens and a spectacular sea view.

Dunbar had a population of fewer than five thousand. Long a center for the grain trade and a market for root vegetables, its harbors frequented by ships destined for Europe and later the American colonies, it became a prosperous market town. Fishing, especially for herring, and whaling flourished to the extent that a second harbor needed to be built in 1844. The merchants and boatbuilders of the town enjoyed good incomes and were able to raise funds to install piped water as early as 1766 and, later, street lighting fueled by whale oil. The town became associated with innovations in maritime technology, with a lighthouse on the Isle of May and a lifeboat service established as early as 1810, along with the lifesaving rocket mechanism that allowed a line to be shot by a small mortar from the shore to a stranded vessel. A local man, a marine engineer, was said to have introduced improvements to the screw propeller and the steam hammer.

Brewing at Belhaven, near the quarry pond where Robert Masterton drowned, went from strength to strength (publicans in Dunbar to this day claim that James Boswell thought the local product the best ale he had ever tasted); so did the extraction of lime and the production of cement and bricks centered there. In Victorian times there were also smaller works manufacturing paper, rope, starch, and soap. But in the later nineteenth century, Dunbar was making its name and much of its income from the natural beauty of its coastline and cliffs, open-air swimming pools, and excellent golf course. It became a fashionable holiday destination, and its hospitality industry blossomed. Well-to-do business families from Glasgow and Edinburgh built impressive houses in which to spend the summer, and frequent train services operated to both these cities.

In short, Dunbar's middle-class life was a far cry from the Gorbals, let alone rented accommodation attached to a factory in Newburgh. How the son of the linen-factory worker met and wooed the daughter of one of the most prosperous and socially prominent Dunbar bourgeois families is unknown. By 1885, and perhaps several years earlier, Robert was working as a shop assis-

No. 1 Delisle Street, Dunbar. (Photograph by Richard Poynder, reproduced by permission.)

tant in Edinburgh, and the couple were living in a rented tenement in Newington. But later that year they moved to a pleasant, solid house at 1 Delisle Street, Dunbar, where their first daughter, Janet, was born. Robert worked for the burgh and stayed in Dunbar for the rest of his life.

His first job on arrival in Dunbar was as the Parish Council's inspector of the poor, a role for which he had experience. But by marrying John Kellie Keir's daughter, he is likely to have been favored in the appointment process. The post required visiting those who asked for or who were felt to require financial support from the town. Robert worked with dedication and made an impression quickly; in June 1886 he was "presented with a testimonial by the committee of the soup kitchen, as well as by a few ladies and gentlemen who took an active interest in its management, as a slight mark of their appreciation of the great assistance he gave them in carrying on the work during the severe weather last winter."[6]

He took on other posts with remuneration, including that of clerk to the cemetery and burgh registrar. His increased eminence brought with it the burgh-financed tenancy of a much larger home for his wife and children, of whom he now had four. It was a substantial Georgian house on North Road named Echo Bank, with a coveted view of the sea and seagulls swooping overhead. He was then able to save sufficient funds to buy a house outright for the first time in his life, in 1901 purchasing an even larger villa in the center of town, Saint Anne's at no. 3 Westgate.

Robert's star continued to rise. He became an elder of the Parish Church, and was largely responsible for its acquisition in 1901 of the excellent organ that played the Handel "Dead March" while his coffin was borne out eleven years later. The purchase followed a long dispute about what architectural improvements should be made to the interior of the church and who should finance them. Robert seems to have played a leading role in the quarrel; the installation of the organ loft controversially required the removal of twenty-eight seats, and he insisted that the instrument be commissioned from the prestigious organ-building company Forster and Andrews, in Hull. It cost two thousand pounds—around a quarter of a million pounds in today's terms. Robert had some keen supporters among the congregation, though, who presented him with "a handsome testimonial" in gratitude for leading the organ campaign.[7]

The newspaper article reporting Robert's death notes that his subsequent major promotion, in 1904 (an event of sufficient importance to be announced in the *Edinburgh Evening News* for September 15), was well deserved: "A man of exceptional business

The interior of the Burgh Hall, Dunbar. (Photograph by Richard Poynder, reproduced by permission.)

capacity, and untiring energy, it was not long before the authorities recognised his valuable business qualities and thorough knowledge of municipal finance, and in course of time he was appointed to the office of Burgh Chamberlain, where he rendered valuable service, recognition of which has been more than once made at town council meetings."

Robert was now in charge of rate collection and the burgh treasury, while retaining the post of inspector of the poor, and his salary was further increased. When the board of the Parish Council recorded his death in the minutes of their meeting on September 27, 1912, his twenty-nine-year service was highly praised. He had been "a man of marked ability," "ever ready in giving counsel and advice," and "in every way a most capable official." His services "contributed largely to the efficiency and marked harmony with which the business was carried through."[8]

The term *harmony* is somewhat surprising, even taking into account officialdom's reluctance to speak ill of the dead, and the council's instruction that an excerpt of the minutes be sent to the widow and family to comfort them "in their affliction." At a service soon after the funeral held in Belhaven Parish Church, near the site of the suicide, the Reverend Melville Stewart sternly enjoined his congregation to stop their mean-minded speculations, but by doing so revealed that Robert was a controversial figure whom some at least of the local community much disliked. Reverend Stewart certainly did not paint a picture of a burgher who created harmony:

> There are certain events and occurrences of which it is impossible to speak, in the face of which wise men become restrained and reticent, and leave to shallow and vulgar minds the morbid satisfaction of idle gossip and conjecture. Such an occurrence was that which last week robbed this community of a man of great public usefulness, whose figure for twenty-eight years had been a most familiar one on our streets, and who—whatever his limitations, and such limitations more or less sad and serious belong to us all—was identified in some way or other with all the best projects and aspirations of this community.

What were these "limitations" which prompted the adjectives "sad and serious"? The minister went into a little more detail:

> Like most men who touch public life at many points, he was bound to create opposition, and I know of no work more calculated to create opprobrium than that of having like him to deal continually with the debased and vagrant poor, in regard to whom any false leniency on his part would have proved him unfit for the unenviable post which he held.[9]

Robert Masterton, clearly, had been far from "lenient" in his treatment of some of the poverty-stricken in the region, perhaps in assessing who among them deserved parochial support. I gain the impression that he was politically conservative, as many who have struggled to escape poverty become in later life. The minister valiantly tried to blame the poor for needing such tough treatment by being debased and vagrant. And he added that he had personal knowledge "that in cases of dire suffering and honest penury, help was often given from his [Robert's] own pocket in relief of such distress." This leaves us with a conundrum. Robert could be mean and perhaps tight-fisted enough with public money to arouse feelings as intense as "opprobrium," and yet in the case of "honest" penury, he was free with his own money. This does not sound so contradictory, however, when we remember the conditions in which he spent his own childhood, seeing different people responding to indigence in different ways, and believing that he had succeeded in escaping poverty himself by honest means and sheer hard work.

The minister offers us one more valuable clue: "It is . . . such things—and not of the days or hours in which his body was ill and his mind distraught—that people should think of today, giving thanks for whatever of good existed in his public career which now has been abruptly ended, and leaving his weakness to his Saviour."

What weakness? Why did he sometimes appear ill in body and distraught in mind? Two of his four children suffered from alcoholism, a terrible, inheritable disease that has, sadly, manifested itself in every subsequent generation descending from him. A picture of a prominent burgher all too often seen drunk in the Dunbar streets is suddenly impossible to banish from the mind's eye. Just as the mighty Ajax was thoroughly humiliated by being seen madly attacking and cursing domesticated livestock, so the burgh officer Robert Masterton had made a show of himself in public, probably while intoxicated. My great-grandfather's wife and her respectable parents must have found this excruciatingly embarrassing.

The impressive Belhaven Parish Church preacher has the kindness to end his sermon offering comfort to Robert's widow and children. Mary Masterton, along with her children Janet, Edith, John ("Jock"), and Ida, all in their teens or early twenties, are "the bereaved family" to whom he extends the congregation's thoughts, "in tenderest sympathy, praying that the Father of the fatherless and the God of all grace may comfort them." The Reverend Melville Stewart knew what a challenge these young people faced in trying to recover from their famous father's infamous demise. And on top of everything else, everyone in the congregation knew that the international situation made war increasingly likely, which would add to the precarity of their situation.

The evidence suggests several factors that could have played a part in Robert Masterton's decision to plunge into a deep pond, perhaps in a state of inebriation; I do not know whether he could swim, or whether he loaded stones into his pockets, but the lakeweed in the pond is dense and tangled and might have dragged him down. Suicide by drowning has never been common. It is relatively slow and painful, and often ends in failure. It accounts for less than 2 percent of incidents, but is more frequent in places like Dunbar where there is easy access to the sea or lakes and ponds. Interestingly, one Stoic metaphor for liberating oneself voluntarily from life is "to swim away from the body as if from a small boat that lets in water." Suicide by drowning occurs occasionally in Greek myth; in one version of her myth, the Theban princess Ino escaped a terrible marriage by leaping into the sea with her son. Deliberate self-drowning is regularly mentioned in ancient sources as a possible means of suicide, for example when the Stoic Seneca exults at the ease with which one can if necessary find a way to end one's life: "The throat may be strangled by a knot, or water may stop one breathing, or the hard ground may crush the skull of one falling headlong to its surface, or inflaming flames may cut off the source of respiration."[10]

Drowning, especially among urban Londoners, was, however, a standard method of suicide in Victorian realist novels. James Thomson's despondent *City of Dreadful Night* (1880), for example, features a drowning in the Thames. Robert Masterton was well read in contemporary fiction, especially in the work of his fellow Scotsman Thomas Carlyle, who meditates at length on suicide in his 1831 best seller *Sartor Resartus.* Other Victorian literary luminaries in whose work suicide looms large include Tennyson, Robert Browning, Matthew Arnold, and George Gissing. A debate in literary journals was instigated by the controversial William Hurrell Mallock's series of articles in *Contemporary Review* and *Nineteenth Century,* which were later assembled into a monograph, *Is Life Worth Living?,* in 1879.[11]

The distinct general sense of fin-de-siècle depression was articulated especially well in Tennyson's dark dramatic monologue "Despair" (1881). Here he speculated about the emotional state of a man contemplating suicide. The narrator and his wife have both tried to drown themselves, since they had come to despise the Calvinist minister who tried to save them by using arguments assuming that there was a providential deity. Only the wife dies. These lines would presumably have struck a chord with Robert Masterton if he had read them, which is likely:

> And the transient trouble of drowning—what was it when match'd with the pains
> Of the hellish heat of a wretched life rushing back thro' the veins?

A similar tone is set by the protagonist of Francis Adams's *A Child of the Age* (1884): "Was I *never* to have rest, peace, comfort, self-sufficiency, call it what you please,—that spiritual sailing with spread canvas before a full and unvarying wind?" Adams killed himself in 1893.[12]

My great-grandfather may have been responding to a sense of despondency that was widespread in the late Victorian and Edwardian eras among the British middle classes. And with the medicalization of suicide, notably in Scotland after the Boer War, he may have seen ending his own life as less morally problematic than he would have done thirty years earlier. Nor did his death require a judicial process; it was not recorded as a suicide. In Scotland, magistrates simply performed a procedure known as a "precognition" in order to discern whether a case needed to be made to the procurator fiscal (public prosecutor) for a suspicious death or if the matter should be allowed to lapse because there was no ground for any judicial process. Since it was decided in Robert Masterton's case that there was no such ground, his death was simply recorded as "drowning" by the local district registrar. And although, strictly speaking, the penalties for willful self-killing in Scotland could still include the forfeiture of movables and some sort of popular or judicial desecration of the corpse, in practice these harsh measures had ceased to be carried out by the early nineteenth century.[13]

Other factors in Robert's decision to end his life may have been the various hardships he endured from childhood on. He was highly intelligent but received no secondary or tertiary education. He suffered multiple bereavements in his early years, then lost his mother at twenty and seems to have been unwilling to stay close to his father after that. He may have faced snobbery from the family into which he married. He may have felt great pressure to compete with his father-in-law's public stature and financial prosperity; John Kellie Keir predeceased him by only three years. Perhaps Robert felt he should have been appointed provost himself; the burgh council underwent some acrimonious political in-fighting during his years as its employee. Most suicidologists accept that self-killing is more prevalent in any given society among the elite, because they can attribute failure only to themselves rather than to social pressures and poverty conspiring to make them fail: "elite" is a relative concept, and within Dunbar and East Lothian society in 1912, Robert Masterton was in the top echelon. His wife may have been "difficult" and have put pressure on him about his drinking.

There was another important aspect to Robert's relationship with his prominent father-in-law. Whereas Robert was an active elder in the Parish Church of Dunbar, his father-in-law was a passionate member and advocate of the Free Church and had long been an elder of that church when Robert Masterton joined the family. Families across Scotland remained riven by the split between "the Kirk" (the historic national Church of Scotland, a Presbyterian and mildly Calvinist organization forged in the Reformation according to the vision of John Knox) and the Free Church. From the moment the Act of Union had come into force in 1707, tensions had mounted over the control of the Church of Scotland by the British government. The Patronage Act of 1712 had transferred the right to choose ministers from the often radical congregations to local lairds, who were usually obedient to the London administration.

In the 1830s, when John Kellie Keir was a child, the rebels had declared that the head of their church should be Jesus Christ and not the British government. By 1843, the tensions had become intolerable and produced the vituperative schism known as the Great Disruption. No fewer than 474 of the more evangelical or proselytizing "low-church" ministers, who were much more extreme Calvinists and believed that all authority resided in the individual, independent community of each congregation, had broken away and formed the Free Church of Scotland. They lost their stipends, their places of worship, and their manses; many were rendered homeless for years. But the new church's leaders were resourceful and soon organized appeals to raise funds to build new churches and homes for their ministers, as well as Free Church schools.[14]

By 1929 the Free Church, which had become the United Free Church, decided to reunify with the Kirk. Yet the religious factionalism in small towns like Dunbar remained extremely acrimonious in the late nineteenth and early twentieth centuries, when John Kellie Keir was living cheek by jowl with his proud and intemperate son-in-law Robert Masterton. There was an ongoing struggle within both local churches between those, like Robert, who advocated reunification, and those, like John, who did not. This conflict would have affected every aspect of the burgh council's business, educational policy, and vision for the town's economy.

John Kellie Keir died in 1909. His obituary in the *Haddingtonshire Courier* of November 14 notes that he had never recovered from the death of his wife a couple of years earlier. But it also contains information that illuminates the sort of issues on which he must have disagreed with his son-in-law. John's religious convictions were strong, and he was vocal in expressing them. The obituary claims that he was one of the greatest public speakers the town had ever heard. He was sufficiently low church to form friendly bonds with the local Wesleyan Methodists and often attended their services. He was active in the left wing of the Liberal Party. But most significant, he was a lifelong and zealous campaigner for the temperance movement.

In his sermon delivered on the Sunday after John's death, the Reverend A. W. Bain spoke thus: "In temperance work, and in every progressive movement, he took a lifelong and deep interest. The last time I heard him speak in public was in opposition to the proposed extension of drinking facilities." Dunbar in the early 1900s was, like much of southern Scotland, blighted by alcohol abuse, and the temperance movement was strong among middle-class nonconformists. There were no fewer than three temperance hotels in the center of the town. But there were many more bars where Robert Masterton could have found alcohol. This must have affected his relationship with his wife's devout and clean-living father.[15]

Robert may also have been worn down by the continuous, daily witnessing of the agony that poverty inflicted on the Scottish underclasses, and frustrated at his inability to improve their situation. Photographs of Dunbar fishing families from the late nineteenth century do suggest that many lived in extreme poverty and squalor. While serving as inspector of the poor he struggled with his own illness and mental distraction, probably related to alcoholism. He got into disputes and made enemies. My impression is of a proud and highly able man who may have felt that he deserved to rise higher professionally or socially than he did, and who faced the transition from midlife to his sixties, an age at which many people feel that doors are closing to them. But here I am speculating just as much as the parishioners rebuked by the worthy ministers. Nobody fully understands why another person chooses suicide, nor "the meaning and the purpose of this dark mystery of providence and personality."

The blow that his death dealt to his wife and children must have been shattering. I believe that all photographs of him were destroyed, in a private pact of *damnatio memoriae,* just as Roman emperors used to order the effacement of all images of their rival predecessors. I conclude this because plentiful photographs of every other member of the Keir family and their in-laws have been preserved. The destruction of portraits may have been a typical response to suicide in Edwardian middle-class households. But then in some ways it had been a typical male suicide.

"Typical" is also the label that Etta Chatterjee, a trained and much-experienced counselor of people planning suicide, has attached to the Sophoclean Ajax's self-destruction. After the protagonist's death, the remainder of the play has little to say about Ajax; rather, it deals with the impact of his suicide on his family, friends, and followers. When I have thought about Robert Masterton's wife, children, siblings, and fellow councilors, citizens, and parishioners at his grim funeral eleven decades ago, Sophocles has always provided me with the thoughts and feelings that I need to imagine—because I cannot know—what took shape in their heads.[16]

Perhaps, although the newspaper report implies that the whole community was astonished by Robert's suicide, the family had known he was plagued by self-destructive impulses and yet had not attempted to curtail his freedom or control the amount of time he spent alone. After Tecmessa discovers Ajax's body, "his blood newly shed, folded around the sword" to bury it from view, the Chorus men immediately reproach themselves for failing to keep their leader "surrounded by friends." They say they have been blind and failed to understand or care for him adequately. Those who are bereaved by suicide usually blame themselves for overlooking signs of despair in the deceased, and for lack of conscientious attention. Ajax's loyal soldiers recall the terrifying bitterness of the hatred he voiced against the Atridae, and they comment, "It was inevitable, inevitable, poor man, that with that stubborn mind of yours, you would fulfil a terrible destiny."

Tecmessa's immediate reaction is one of desolation: she is destroyed, "utterly razed to the ground," like a besieged city. She is fully aware that Ajax's greatness in life makes his ignominious end seem far more tragic: how the mighty one is fallen. She immediately covers him with a large cloth since, she says, nobody who loves him could bear to see the signs of his self-inflicted injuries. This was a famous gesture, much reproduced in ancient artefacts which celebrate the pain and care of the bereaved woman rather than the suicidal man. I do not know whether my grandfather's body was seen by his surviving family, but I am sure the sight would have been almost unbearable.

When the Chorus men try to comfort the howling Tecmessa, she retorts that they can hold whatever opinion they like, but only *she* feels the full extent of the grief. Since Ajax had such powerful enemies, she also feels terrible vulnerability now that she has nobody to protect her, as all widows, and perhaps most of all widows tainted by the public shame of suicide, must feel in a traditional patriarchal society.

Ajax's half-brother Teucer is equally distraught. He knew his brother's personality and laments his "over-hasty," "precipitate," tragic act; he almost immediately worries about his nephew, Ajax's son, and sends Tecmessa to find him. Then, alone with the Chorus, Teucer delivers a heartrending speech anticipating the repercussions that the suicide will inflict on him personally. He is not a full Salaminian citizen, since he was the son by Telamon of a foreign princess, the Trojan Hesione; nor did he share Ajax's warrior status as mighty hoplite (foot soldier), since he was skilled instead at the slightly less prestigious art of archery.

He asks for the corpse to be uncovered, even though Ajax's face seems to him to be full "of bitter bravado"; the sight of it "is truly the most painful thing my eyes have ever seen." With scathing sarcasm he remarks to the corpse of his half-brother that Telamon, their father, is hardly likely to welcome Teucer back in Salamis "with a kindly face and manner" if he returns bearing this shocking news. He knows this because, he says, Telamon is a man who rarely smiles even when things are going his way.

Teucer describes the unpleasant things that families responding to the suicide of a favorite member say: his father will compare Teucer negatively with his brother, calling him illegitimate, cowardly, and perhaps to blame for the suicide. We discover, too, from whom Ajax inherited or learned his fierce and hasty disposition: Telamon is "a man of difficult temper, severe in old age, who lightly starts angry conflicts for negligible reasons." The apple does not fall far from the tree. Teucer also tries to understand what has happened in terms of the fateful chain of cause and effect that killed so many warriors at Troy.

But Ajax's suicide has created a more immediate problem for his hapless half-brother. Menelaus arrives, and tells Teucer that Ajax will be forbidden burial since he had tried to assault both Menelaus and his brother Agamemnon. Teucer stands his ground and sees the imperious Spartan king off. Then he leaves Tecmessa and Eurysaces kneeling by the corpse, taking up the positions of suppliants, having cut off locks of their hair in mourning. He orders the Chorus to protect them while he absents himself to find a place for the burial.

Agamemnon now arrives, furious that Teucer is insisting on burying Ajax. After a vicious argument, Teucer states simply that if Ajax's corpse is to be discarded ignominiously, it will be accompanied by the corpses of Tecmessa, Eurysaces, and himself. They will die defending Ajax's body. Even Agamemnon would hesitate to incur the divine wrath that slaughtering three suppliants would entail.

Affairs have reached an impasse. At this point, Odysseus appears and acts as mediator, talking humane good sense. Of course, Ajax must be given an honorable burial. Odysseus cites three reasons. First, Ajax, whatever happened to him latterly, had been a great soldier and done important service for the Greeks. In addition, it is against divine law to refuse a human burial: "When a good man is dead, there is no justice in doing him harm, not even if you hate him." Most important, death comes to everyone, and we need to treat the dead in the way in which we want to be treated ourselves. Odysseus relinquishes his long-term hostility toward Ajax, and even offers to participate in the funeral.

One later source suggests that there were some doubts about whether Ajax could be allowed the hero's honorable cremation, or whether the suicide weapon—his sword—should be buried alongside him. But in Sophocles' play, the question at issue is not a religious one. It is not even asked whether Ajax as a suicide should

Tecmessa, Eurysaces, and Teucer with the corpse of Ajax, aquatint etching printed by Carl Russ for the publisher Johann Friedrich Frauenholz, ca. 1807-11. (Reproduced with the permission of the British Museum.)

be deprived of burial rites. The problem is that his enemies try to prevent them. Odysseus's humane words, however, speak loudly across the centuries. A man who has served his people well does not annul those services because he is struck with one calamity and ends his own life. Like Robert Masterton, Ajax deserved an honorable send-off and recognition by his community. Mercifully, wherever Robert was buried, he was given one.[17]

Chapter 5

THE GRANDMOTHER'S TALE

IN ONE OF THE SADDEST ANCIENT STORIES ABOUT suicide, a daughter's grief at her father's death causes her to hang herself; the family dog then imitates his mistress, dying of grief. The pain inflicted on relatives by suicide is transferred to the household pet. The story comes near the end of an epic about the wine god Dionysus by a poet called Nonnus, who lived in Panopolis, a Greek-speaking city in Egypt, in the fifth century CE. He may have been a Christian, but he reveled in the old pagan myths.

Dionysus, the tale goes, was on a world mission to introduce the vine, and the practice of drinking wine, to all humanity. He eventually arrived in Attica, the countryside around Athens. He sought out the gardener who knew the most about the cultivation of trees. The gardener, Icarius, lived in a humble cottage with his daughter Erigone, who looked after their herd of cows.

The old man took enthusiastically to the wine Dionysus bestowed on him, just as Robert Masterton was probably to take to alcohol. Afterward Icarius taught his countrymen how to grow vines and make wine from the grapes. Everyone appreciated the emotionally anesthetic effects of the delicious drink—its ability to relieve the mind of anxiety. But alcohol, whatever its pleasures, is fraught with danger. One day some local peasants drank far too much, lost their reason, and turned against Icarius, attacking him violently. He died of his injuries. In his last words he expressed his concern for his daughter, who, he believed, would not be able to survive the grief she was about to undergo.

The next day the peasants were appalled to discover that they had killed Icarius, and they gave him a proper burial. Icarius's ghost then visited Erigone in a dream, coming close to her and showing her his wounds. Erigone woke up, distraught, tore her hair and breast with her fingernails, and went to look for her father. Eventually another gardener showed her Icarius's tomb:

> The girl, listening, became crazed but with a sober kind of madness.
> She tore out locks of her hair and placed them on the beloved tomb,
> a maiden unveiled, barefoot, soaking her clothing
> as her spontaneous tears welled up ceaselessly.
> Her lips remained sealed in wordless silence
> for a time. But Erigone's companion, her dog, who felt the same,
> whimpered and howled alongside the girl as she mourned,
> grieving with her as she grieved. In her distraction,
> she dashed up to a tall tree. She attached a noose to it,
> tying it tightly round her neck. Swinging in the air, she
> died a self-inflicted death by hanging;
> both feet twitched, quivering like a dancer's.
> And so she met the death she willed on herself. But her dog
> wheeled repeatedly around her, howling sorrowfully,
> an animal dropping tears of compassion from his eyes.

This intelligent dog protected Erigone's dangling corpse from beasts of prey, then pointed her out to wayfarers, who took her down and buried her. Nonnus tells us that he even helped them dig her grave, grubbing at the soil with his paws. The travelers soon went on their way,

> but because of his love for Erigone, the dog alone remained,
> beside the tomb, and himself met his death voluntarily.

In some sources, the dog hurls himself from a cliff; Nonnus, on the other hand, seems to imply that he starved himself to death. If you look into the night sky, you can still see this doomed family. Zeus pitied them. He turned the dog into Sirius, the brilliant star that heralds the long, hot dog days of summer. Erigone joined the constellation Virgo, and Icarius joined Boötes, the constellation of the plow.[1]

Nonnus has transferred the pain of the family member bereaved by suicide to the loyal dog. He has even made the dog carry out an imitative suicide. The ancient Greeks knew a good deal about the effects of death, and suicide, upon those who love the deceased. Nonnus's story is one of the clearest expressions of this agonizing emotional understanding.

This story always makes me think of my grandmother—not only because she mourned her father grievously and eventually killed herself. She also loved dogs. There is a photograph of the Masterton family in about 1913, not long after her father's death, in which she sits with a small, shaggy black dog on her knee. I even dimly remember her telling me the story of Greyfriars Bobby, a black Skye terrier who became famous in Victorian Edinburgh. Until his death on January 14, 1872, he sat for fourteen years in Greyfriars Kirkyard beside the grave of his deceased owner, a police nightwatchman named John Gray. My mother once took me to see Bobby's commemorative statue on the corner of Candlemaker Row.

One of the most searing anecdotes about my mother's relationship with her parents also involves a puppy. When Brenda, my mother, was about eight years old, her mother, Edith, realized that her child was lonely. One day, when her husband, Walter, was away, she bought herself and her daughter a puppy. He was a black Skye terrier, and they adored him. But when Walter returned after a few weeks, he took one look at the beloved dog, and simply said, "*That* has to go." The puppy disappeared overnight. My mother never forgave Walter, and perhaps neither did *her* mother.

This story shocked me as a child. My mother rarely spoke about her father's emotional cruelty. But the incident gives a penetrating insight into Edith's marriage. The innocent comfort that a depressed woman could derive from sharing a pet with her lonely child was not permitted them. I do not know why Walter objected to the dog. But I am not surprised that my grandmother found herself unable to love such a man. And yet she had given up any chance of personal or professional fulfilment to marry him.

Edith Henderson was born in Dunbar on December 3, 1889, the second daughter of Robert and Mary Masterton, who were then in their early thirties. They lived in a succession of comfortable middle-class villas. Edith would have known both her maternal grandparents well, the eminent town councilor John Kellie Keir and his wife, Janet, who performed her duties as what the local newspapers called First Lady of Dunbar with alacrity during the Royal Jubilee celebrations, when Edith was seven. They lived nearby and survived into her teens.

Edith's school-leaving certificate indicates that she left Higher Grade Public School in the Dunbar Burgh in 1908, passing with high marks in Latin and French. She was two or three years older than the other pupils who left that year; most of them were born in 1891 or 1892, but I have found no explanation of the age difference. Her sister Ida left the year after, in 1909, even though she was more than three years younger, with less distinguished marks, failing in math and French. Perhaps Edith's academic work was already being impacted by the depressive illness affecting other members of the family. Her father may have been succumbing to the alcoholic melancholia that led to his death; her mother may well have been depressed, having lost both her mother and her uncle Peter Keir in 1907. Her father was already sickening (she lost him too in 1909).

In the first few years of the century, however, constant alterations were being made to the implementation of the still relatively

Edith Masterton in 1910. (Author's collection.)

new Scottish school-leaving certificate, which was issued only to students who had attended a full course of secondary education, including mathematics or a science and a foreign language, for at least four years. Until 1908 confusion remained over the number of subjects required for university matriculation, and this uncertainty may have delayed Edith's completion of her formal schooling.

Of all Robert and Mary's four children, Edith was by far the most academically talented. Although her family was well read, she was the first to progress from school to university. Her devotion to her father suggests that he may have channeled into his clever second daughter his own frustrations as a highly intelligent man who felt he had not fulfilled his maximum potential. But she also learned from her mother to be an outstanding needlewoman, and she had a theatrical bent. Her younger brother John ("Jock"), the only Masterton whom I remember well, described the amateur theatricals she led in their Dunbar nursery, usually acting out romantic scenes from novels by Sir Walter Scott.

A faded photograph taken at the premises of Ben Brown, 16 Brougham Street, Edinburgh, shows her reveling as a child of about eight in the type of theatrical scene that commercial photographers offered their clients: she smiles conspiratorially out from a rowing boat, wielding the oar with some alacrity. She is flanked by mannequins representing chaperones in late-Victorian straw hats, one reading a newspaper, and behind her a painted backdrop depicts a riverbank. Another photograph taken a year or two later shows a charismatic teenager with a direct if enigmatic gaze and an upright posture.

We next meet Edith as an undergraduate at Edinburgh University, where she entered the four-year degree course in English and Latin. Women had been able to attend lectures at this university starting in 1867, but only a few of them graduated. Edith attended the lectures on English literature given by the world-famous professor George Saintsbury and was deeply impressed by him. By the time she heard him lecture, he was a grand old man and something of a cult figure, who appeared in affectionate cartoons in the student press. One student described him in 1904 as a "forard-set figire [sic] loose-clad in the gloomy gown . . . not a dull moment in the hour . . . with a genius for interesting, annoying and instructing his hearers." A radical young student,

Edith Masterton as a child. (Author's collection.)

A. S. Neill, who was a contemporary of Edith's and went on to found a famous school, rebelled against the great man's views, but nevertheless praised him in a 1912 editorial in the undergraduate newspaper *Student* for his approachability, kindness, and humor.[2]

Undoubtedly the most formative event of Edith's life occurred during her student days. She worshipped her father, and when he killed himself mid-August, she was probably at home in Dunbar and would have seen him the morning of the day he died. Since Edith was the most able of Mary's children, her mother leaned on her second daughter both emotionally and in terms of practical organization. Edith must have had a great deal to cope with on top of processing her own shock, loss, grief, and public embarrassment. But she had not completed her degree, and she needed to return to the university and continue to attend Saintsbury's lectures.

One of her principal university textbooks was Saintsbury's celebrated *Loci Critici: Passages Illustrative of Critical Theory and Practice from Aristotle Downwards,* first published in 1903. Edith's copy of this classic collection contains hundreds of her marginal comments, scrawled in ink with a fountain pen, as well as emphatic underscorings. As I read through the passages of Aristotle's *Poetics* and *Rhetoric* that she clearly studied with deep concentration, I felt the hair stand up on the back of my neck, since I had spent so much time thinking about these identical sentences. An idea of what she found most exciting about literature is revealed in the underscorings in the excerpts from more recent critics, such as William Wordsworth and Matthew Arnold; most of these passages concern the ability of literature to express imagination, passion, and emotion. Edith seems to have been particularly struck by Arnold's statement that what is most fit for poetical representation is what leads the reader to "the elementary part of our nature, to our passions, that which is great and passionate."[3]

Inside the back cover, in her slanting inky characters, a single poem is copied out in its entirety. She does not give a title or author, but the capacities of online search engines have allowed me to track these down. The poet's name was Arthur Stringer, a Canadian writer (1894–1950) more famous for his biography of Rupert Brooke than his own largely unremarkable poems. The poem my grandmother took the time to copy was published in the Kansas newspaper *The Hutchinson Daily News* on Wednesday, June 22, 1910, in the "Society" column. It is titled "Out of the Mists of Dream":

> Out of the mists of Dream, where Regret is crowned with gold
> Wherewith the autumn of yearning the years wax never old,
> As the sunset to the silence, as the starlight seeks the sea,
> You and your twilight eyes still beckon and turn to me.
> Turn with a touch of the glory, where golden skylines gleam.
> Turn to me still through the gloaming, out of the mists of Dream.
>
> Out of the mists of Dream, where the seasons know no change,
> Where, should a love endure, all sorrow and loss are strange;
> Steadfast unto, and tender and ever true,
> Broods the unaltering glory, the sad, Glad eyes of you—
> You who have called and waited, as the ocean calls the stream.
> And my soul has sought and drawn you, out of the mists of Dream![4]

If Edith inscribed the poem before her father's death, it offers insights into her introspective emotional life and her aesthetic tastes. But if, as seems far more likely to me, she copied it because it spoke to her after his death, then several of its phrases seem relevant to her probable state of mind. It is a poem about summoning, via a dream, someone whom the subject voice of the poem has lost, but who is waiting for the one left behind: "should a love endure, all sorrow and loss are strange." The stress on the sea, the skyline, and the twilight are also suggestive of Robert Masterton's

Edith Masterton's graduation photograph. (Author's collection.)

lonely, watery demise that summer night on the southern banks of the Firth of Forth.

Despite her shocking bereavement, Edith did graduate. She achieved high average marks in history, in Latin, and on the teaching proficiency certificate, and overall a second-class degree. But in English literature and English language she graduated *Insigni cum Laude* (with notable praise, i.e., with distinction). It was to be the proudest achievement of her life; it must have been excruciating not to be able to tell her father.

During the war, Edith worked as a volunteer nurse in Edinburgh, as a V.A.D. with the local Red Cross Voluntary Aid Detachment branch; she there met her friend for life, Norah ("Nonie") Walker, who was doing the same. The two were among many hundred young women volunteers, mostly from middle-class backgrounds (the pay was pitiful), working at the military medical centers. These included Craiglockhart Hospital (where shellshocked officers including the poets Siegfried Sassoon and Wilfred Owen were treated) and the 2nd Scottish General Hospital in the former Craigleith Poorhouse, which had been taken over by the Territorial Force to provide more than a thousand beds to injured servicemen of lower ranks.[5]

In the 1920–21 census Edith is identified as living alone at 11c Leven Terrace, Edinburgh, a typical solid-Victorian residential terrace flat; I was told that after the war she taught English for some years in a prestigious city center school. In a photograph taken around this time she looks happier than in any other: attractive and fashionably dressed, her hair bobbed, a New Woman of the flapper generation.

No doubt she relished the right to vote which had finally become hers, once she reached her thirtieth birthday, by the Representation of the People Act 1919, shortly before the photograph was taken. But when her mother died at the age of only sixty-one in 1920, eight years after her father's suicide, she may have

Edith Masterton, c. 1921. (Author's collection.)

felt intensely alone. She seems to have decided on marriage as a solution.

Scotland, however, suffered from an acute shortage of eligible bachelors after the carnage of the trenches. She settled, with reluctance, as my mother implied, for Walter Henderson.

He was an up-and-coming Glasgow lawyer, like Edith the first member of his family to go to a university. He had read law at Glasgow. But he came from commerce—a shopkeeping family that she regarded, being inclined toward snobbery, as somewhat socially and educationally inferior to her own. But it was also decidedly wealthier. He was amusing company, but very short and physically unattractive. My mother told me that Edith did not love him.

She gave up work after they married on September 3, 1923, although the school where she taught had no formal requirement to do so, in accordance with the social pressures on middle-class women at the time and their internalized patriarchal values. But the pressure to view oneself primarily as a wife and mother places impossible burdens on women: as the psychoanalytic feminist scholar Jacqueline Rose has written, it is "one of the most striking aspects of the discourse on mothering that the idealization does not let up as the reality of the world makes the ideal harder for the mother to meet." My grandmother's predicament always reminds me of a poignant poem by Agathias in the *Palatine Anthology,* in which the poet expresses his understanding of the plight of girls, adopting their voice in the first person plural:

> Youths do not suffer as much
> as we do, tender-hearted females.
> They have friends of the same age
> to whom they can confidently speak
> of their problems and sorrows.
> They have games to make them happy;
> they can roam the streets and look around
> at all the pictures. But for us, on the contrary,
> it's not even permissible to see the light of day.
> We wither away inside our homes, the prey of gloomy thoughts.[6]

In Euripides' *Medea* the heroine, who has been abandoned by her husband, Jason, makes similar complaints about the caged life of women, in this case married women. They must have sex with their husbands on demand, and they are not permitted a social life. While their husbands have many activities and companions outside the house, wives are almost entirely dependent on their husbands for conversation and stimulation:

> And if after making these enormous efforts
> our husband cohabits with us without struggling violently under the
>   yoke,
> we are enviable. But otherwise, death is better.

What a difference it might have made to Edith to be able to pursue a career that befitted her poise, articulacy, and well-trained brain. She would not have withered away at home, the eternal prey of gloomy thoughts.

Walter Henderson had a substantial income, and they lived in bourgeois prosperity in a grand villa on Dalziel Drive in Pollokshields, Glasgow, with servants and a cook. Two years after they wed, their daughter Brenda, my mother, was born. Not long afterward Edith lost a baby boy, although I never discovered whether he was stillborn or died soon after birth.

Edith was intelligent, and in her periods of relative wellness read avidly. I have inherited many of her books, in which she has neatly inscribed her signature and often marked sentences or verses with a pencil. She had read almost every word of her three-volume *Chamber's Encyclopedia of English Literature* (1901), with its sumptuous dark-blue tooled-leather binding. There are many elegant hardback copies of canonical drama, especially Shakespeare, the Jacobeans, Ben Jonson, and George Bernard Shaw; English and Scottish poetry, especially work by Milton, Burns, Keats, Tennyson, and Browning; canonical fiction, including Elizabeth Gaskell,

George Eliot, Walter Scott, and Thomas Hardy. German and French literary criticism and fiction in translation are also abundant.

My mother once or twice talked about Edith's relationships with two of her siblings. Edith's sister Ida was a pretty, troubled character, said to have been addicted to alcohol and card games. Edith thought Ida somewhat superficial but also great fun. Ida married a naval doctor called Maurice Moore and moved away from the town. Ida's twin John ("Jock"), on the other hand, was a hero for Edith. Unlike her father, he had conquered alcoholism, after drinking far too much for three years following his return to Scotland as a survivor of the trenches.

Jock had been theater mad since childhood; he later recalled slipping out of his bedroom window as a boy to sneak into the summer shows put on by the traveling players who visited Dunbar to entertain holidaymakers. When his father killed himself in 1912, Jock, Robert's only son, found one positive aspect to the family tragedy. He sensed an opportunity to escape the Kirk-dominated small-town atmosphere of Dunbar, packed his bags, and went to Edinburgh. He told his mother that he was training for the ministry, though everyone knew that he was terrible at Greek and Hebrew, at that time requirements for ordination. In reality he was spending every waking hour with a hugely popular amateur dramatic club in Leith, writing sketches and one-act plays as well as acting and stage managing. The Windsor Club's productions toured Scottish towns and even made marginal profits.[7]

Only twenty when war broke out, Jock was excited about joining the Lothian and Border Horse, and was proud to have been the youngest lieutenant in charge of dispatch riders. He was transferred to the 44th Siege Battery of the Royal Garrison Artillery on the day it was formed, July 12, 1915, at Sheerness in Kent. He was then sent to the western front to man massive railway howitzers, entrenched in deep dugouts. The experience of firing up to sixty-eight rounds a day continuously for the three months of the Somme offensive left men with damaged hearing for life, along with damaged nerves. It was even worse during the attack on Vimy Ridge, when the role of the heavy howitzers was newly defined as providing counter-battery fire even for well-protected enemy guns. Incessant twenty-four-hour exposure to exploding artillery shells became a fact of life.

Jock was blown up in 1916, receiving damage to both arms. He recovered physically, though not neurologically, and was sent back into action, only to be blown up again. He suffered his entire remaining life not only from difficulty in walking steadily but from what was then called shell-shock and is now more often called posttraumatic stress disorder. Recent research suggests, however, that PTSD is not solely a psychological condition; blast force from battlefield explosions leaves distinctive—and permanent—lesions on the brain. For two years Jock lost the power of speech (a frequent problem for Somme survivors) and drank himself into a stupor almost every day. But in 1921 he managed to pull himself together, drank the last glass of whisky of his life, and talked his way into the post of manager of the King's Theatre in Edinburgh. He was successful and popular; he modernized the repertoire, hired high-profile actors, and doubled the size of the regular audiences. Edith went to all the plays and shows he commissioned until her marriage, when she moved to Glasgow, and often visited him afterward.[8]

Jock joined the Edinburgh Lyceum in 1928. In 1938 he was invited to transfer to the King's Theatre Hammersmith, but the London move was not a success. As soon as World War II broke out, he took early retirement and lived in quiet seclusion with his wife (they had no children) in a bungalow on the Edinburgh ring road. My family visited them every time we went to Scotland, at least three times a year. I remember him as a kind, charming, slender middle-aged man with a mild but persistent tremor affecting his whole body. My mother loved him dearly and was impressed that he had managed to abstain completely from alcohol since the early 1920s. I can remember her weeping for several days after he died, of natural causes, in 1966, four years after the death of his sister Edith.

Despite her two strong and supportive relationships, with Jock and Nonie Walker, my grandmother Edith's life, my mother admitted, was blighted by long bouts of severe depression. She sought help from the most expensive doctors and psychiatrists, spent time in residential institutions, tried various forms of medication, and underwent electroconvulsive therapy (ECT), but all to no avail. She spent much of her life lying on her bed in a darkened room with the curtains closed, smoking but not drinking more than a single cocktail each evening, and weeping constantly. Throughout her childhood, my mother dreaded being summoned to Edith's bedside, preferring her own company and that of the radio.

In her better spells, when she was able to get up, dress, and seek out company, Edith found ways of escaping her unloved husband, who was, in fact, rarely home. He was a workaholic, and on top of his law practice served on numerous trusts and charitable bodies. His favorite cause was the historic Glasgow Royal Infirmary, founded in 1791 with a Royal Charter "for the Relief of the Indigent Persons laboring under Poverty and Disease" and funded chiefly by subscribers, members of the professional and merchant classes keen on burnishing their philanthropic credentials. The city's population had risen dramatically during the eighteenth century, and disease was rife.

The infirmary had been hit with severe financial and staffing problems during World War I and the influenza epidemic that followed it. As a board member, Walter Henderson played a leading role in increasing subscriptions and raising revenue, some of which was used to build much-needed residences for nurses and to modernize the facilities. He was also active in the reforms of procedures and policies led by the enterprising Dr. John Cowan in the 1930s, when the infirmary became the pride of western Scotland's medical services. During World War II, despite the extra challenges, the hospital acquired an excellent new Out-Patient Department and X-ray equipment. A neurosurgical clinic was opened, under Dr. Sloan Robertson, and it was there that I suspect Edith later received her ECT treatment. But in 1945, at the end of the war, the Finance Committee reported that resources were near exhaustion.

The situation was reversed only in 1947, when the exceptionally competent Walter took over as honorary treasurer and succeeded in securing a massive maintenance grant from the Department of Health. This kept the infirmary running until the U.K. prime minister Clement Attlee announced in a broadcast to the nation on Sunday, July 4, 1948, that "this day makes history," and the National Health Service was launched. Walter had been one of its most enthusiastic advocates. His services to the Lanarkshire public were recognized by the award of an OBE in 1952. His philanthropy did not extend to showing kindness to his wife and child.[9]

Edith frequently traveled to Edinburgh to visit Jock, or to Fife to stay with her best friend Nonie. Nonie was a resolute single woman who responded with characteristic high spirits to the shortage of potential husbands by becoming a career teacher and financially independent, serving as the deeply loved headmistress of the primary school in Elie, Fife, for decades. Nonie set up home with her invalid sister Mabel, whom she looked after devotedly, in a house on the High Street, which my mother eventually inherited, and which my sister Nicola and her husband now own. Nonie was effectively my granny throughout my childhood, invariably a kind and humorous one. She had been a rock for her depressed friend Edith. My mother loved the periods when she and her mother would stay in Elie: Edith would laugh in Nonie's company as she never did elsewhere.

The other way that Edith spent time, when not too depressed to leave the marital mansion, was by staying at luxurious hotels across mainland Britain. My mother, who was expected to travel as Edith's companion, mentioned to me over the years a hotel in Cornwall, one in Llandudno, and several in the Scottish Highlands. They would stay in these hotels for weeks, which must have been expensive, but Walter was earning well and willing to pay. Edith used to sparkle socially, spend hours talking to other guests, play card games, and maintain cordial relationships with hoteliers and waiting staff. There is no suggestion that she ever had an affair or even wanted one, but she liked the company of attractive men. Everyone was far happier when Walter and Edith were apart.

When my mother left home to study law at Saint Hugh's College, Oxford, Edith was resentful. She required her sensible, practical, stoical daughter to act as her constant companion and, all too often, psychiatric nurse. Feeling abandoned in Glasgow, she simply packed her numerous expensive suitcases and hatboxes and moved into a hotel in North Oxford. She then parasitically invaded my mother's social life.

After graduating from Oxford, my mother did not return to Glasgow. When she married my father, a man from a working-class London family, Edith was further displeased and for a time cut off all contact. My mother said she had named me Edith in part to try to win back her mother's favor, and the ploy worked. But in the summer of 1962, exactly fifty years after her father's suicide, Edith made at least one abortive attempt on her own life. (Research has shown that the anniversary of the death of a father is a date favored for suicide attempts.) I do not know what method she used.[10]

I vaguely recall visiting the house in Pollokshields a couple of weeks later; my sister remembers playing then with Edith's needlework box. My mother, with a house removal to sort out because my father had just been appointed lecturer in theology at Nottingham University, drove all the way north from Birmingham with her three small children in tow. There were as yet no motorways, and the vehicle was an elderly, fifth-hand Bentley, which she had to crank by hand to get started.

With Walter's permission, my mother hired for Edith a female companion/nurse, who was instructed never to leave the depressed woman's side, and to intervene if she attempted self-harm. My dismal grandmother and her chaperone were packed off on a recuperative vacation to a hotel in Largs, a fashionable seaside resort on the North Ayrshire shore. My mother could not and would not drop everything to stay for long periods, hundreds of miles away from her husband, every time her invalid mother summoned her.

But at the hotel, Edith evaded the companion's supervision long enough to leap out of her bedroom window on an upper floor. It was a Monday evening, just as her father's death had been. Like her father, she died beside a beach in a resort on one of the southern coasts of Scotland. Experts have demonstrated the frequency of suicides taking place in a similar place and manner to those previously performed by close family members.[11]

She was found dead on the ground outside the hotel early in the morning. Nobody alive knows why her chaperone did not alert anyone to her disappearance. Her death certificate says that the cause of her death was exposure. Her older sister Janet died in Edinburgh, apparently of natural causes but almost certainly hastened by shock and grief, the following Sunday, October 7, 1962.

The hotel where Edith died was one in which she had often stayed, the glamorous Marine and Curlinghall Hotel. It had been founded by Catherine Logan, a businesswoman who had made a small fortune in the retail drapery business in Glasgow. She may well have become friends with Edith Henderson, whose father-in-law was a successful shop owner. Logan bought the ornate three-story mansion with Gothic turrets in Largs and opened it as the Barra House Hotel, soon renamed the Marine Hotel. It swiftly acquired a reputation for excellence, attracting not only the well-heeled from western Scotland but, especially during World War II, aristocrats from England who were thrilled by the ample and delicious local products served to them—small game, venison, seafood, raspberries, oatcakes with Lanark Blue cheese, or Cairnsmore, made from sheep's milk—in the elegant oak-paneled dining-room. It was also much frequented by senior members of the armed forces.

After the war, the Logan family also acquired the hotel next door, the Curlinghall. This was a magnificent house which had been built in 1812 to accommodate Scotland's first artificial curling pond, later replaced with tennis courts. Its large grounds included a rose garden and a vinery, a grotto, a fish pond, a darkroom for photography activities, and a bowling green. When the two premises were joined architecturally in 1953, the hotel boasted 90 bedrooms and 350 dining places. The imposing combined edifice provided lovely gardens, a putting course, televisions, a cinema, a billiards table, gift and clothing shops, powder rooms, telephone kiosks, a cocktail lounge, and a ballroom with a fully sprung floor where the hotel's famous Saturday night dinner dances were attended by as many as six hundred guests. It was the obvious choice of venue for the official dinners held by the local council or the yacht club. Queen Elizabeth and Prince Philip had been welcomed outside on a visit in 1958. But by the early hours of October 1, 1962, none of these attractions mattered to Edith Henderson, who was out of her mind with despair.

The previous pages of this chapter contain the sum total of what my mother told me about her mother, heavily supplemented by my own more recent inquiries. The account is assembled from tiny fragments in disparate conversations occurring over half a century. The picture they paint is profoundly tragic. The almost complete absence of information I possess about Edith from the

The Marine and Curlinghall Hotel, Largs. (Author's collection.)

1920s to my birth in March 1959 perhaps speaks for itself. Until the autumn of 2016 I knew very little about my grandmother. My mother, Brenda, had occasionally mentioned something about her; I learned to seize on these rare moments of candor and press for more information. But my probing invariably made her clam up and change the subject, with a tight-lipped smile that forbade further questioning.

There may have been little to say. Edith had no profession, no career, and few friends. Her only serious hobbies were solitary ones—reading and needlework. She enjoyed good food, but did not cook since there were servants for that; during World War II she was apparently adept at circumventing the rations system to acquire fresh game and vegetables from contacts in the Highlands.

She did love the theater, and took my mother to every Shakespeare production available in southern Scotland, including those commissioned in Edinburgh by her brother Jock; she also, rather surprisingly for a female member of the haute bourgeoisie, enjoyed watching live football (soccer) matches, especially the raucous showdowns between Celtic and Rangers, and would drag my mother along. Only one child in the family meant few birthdays to celebrate; Brenda was partly educated at home by governesses, which compounded her seclusion. Since servants were sent to accompany Brenda to and from the school she did attend for a year or two, the exclusive girls' private school Laurel Bank, there were not even school runs and chats in the playground to break up Edith's days.

Edith had certainly been diagnosed with depressive illness by the 1930s. As far as I am aware, she was never hospitalized by it before World War II. Electroconvulsive therapy, which was introduced after the war, was less painful than many cinematic representations suggest, but it could certainly be a frightening experience. Although it has been effective for some people, it made no difference to my grandmother. More alarming, I have a faint memory of my mother saying that a leucotomy had been performed on Edith in the 1950s; this procedure often resulted in diminished intellectual and cognitive powers and loss of ability to relate emotionally to what other people were going through. She did not, as far as I am aware, undertake psychoanalysis or psychotherapy. Perhaps she realized how diminished were her mental powers: an ancient Roman orator named Messala Corvinus became depressed when he lost his memory and ability to finish sentences at the age of seventy-two, the age at which Edith died; when he also contracted cancer, he made away with himself.[12]

Edith died too early to benefit from the tricyclic antidepressants and subsequently selective serotonin reuptake inhibitors (SSRIs) that have transformed the lives of so many people since the 1960s, including myself; medication for depression in her day had scarcely advanced beyond Hippocrates' recommendation that those with an urge to hang themselves should take mandragora.

In fact, her treatments were probably far less enlightened than those advocated by the physician Asclepiades in the early first century BCE. He recommended comforting the patient and cultivating mental balance through music, bathing, and fresh air. He objected to the crude vocabulary used to dismiss people with emotional disturbances as "insane," and insisted on distinguishing between chronic and temporary mental illness.[13]

Research into the effect of a father's premature death on his daughter reveals certain patterns that are suggestive for the impact that Robert Masterton's suicide had on the young adult Edith. The impact is far worse when the mother is either emotionally inexpressive or, on the other hand, overwhelmed with grief, and therefore does not allow the daughter space to express her own pain. Daughters often blame themselves for their father's decision to die. They are particularly liable to recurrent bouts of grief throughout their lives, especially around anniversaries or on emotional occasions. Daughters of men who die by suicide dwell introspectively on their fathers' motives. They are likely to mold an idealized picture of their fathers in their minds, creating unreachable expectations of other men, and leaving them dissatisfied in romantic or marital relationships. They avoid facing the problematic aspects of their fathers' personalities and concentrate on compassionate identification.[14]

No doubt Edith thought a great deal about suicide in Shakespeare, Jacobean and Restoration drama, and the nineteenth-century poetry and fiction she so enjoyed. But for me as a classicist, the poetry that has helped me think about the psychological pain she must have been enduring that led her to kill herself at seventy-two is far older.

There is no evidence that any tragic love affair was involved in her self-destructive impulses—the main motive in the suicides of women in classical myths: Phaedra, whose love for Hippolytus was not requited; Phyllis, who mistakenly believed her beloved

Demophoon would never return; Dido, who was abandoned by Aeneas. Nor do I know of any dramatic or scandalous incident in her life that Edith might have been ashamed of, such as the events that accounted for the suicides of ancient heroines such as Pelopia and Harpalyce, who committed incest with their fathers, or Byblis and Canace on account of incestuous desires for or actual incest with a brother. Perhaps more relevant is the case of Leda, so horrified by what she perceived to be the bad behavior of her daughter Helen that she killed herself.[15]

Edith had also lost a son. The loss of her baby may illuminate why she adored her fellow Scot and Edinburgh University alumnus J. M. Barrie's *Peter Pan,* originally a play (1904), in which the death of small boys figures large, a response in part to the expiry, when Barrie was six years old, of his older brother David in an iceskating accident: the lost boys are "the children who fall out of their prams when the nurse is looking the other way." Some classical women destroy themselves in despair after a son's death, for example, Neaera, the legendary daughter of a notorious robber named Autolycus who lived on Mount Parnassus, when her nephew killed her son Hippothous. In Euripides' version of the story of Jocasta—as opposed to that of Sophocles—the queen did not kill herself for many years after the truth came out. She stayed alive, the matriarch of Thebes, until after her sons had slaughtered each other in battle. When she heard the news, she ran to the field of combat, snatched up a sword, and only then dispatched herself and died with her arms embracing the two of them. The last scene of this play, *Phoenician Women,* enacts the emotional impact of this suicide on the surviving family members—her brother Creon, her daughter Antigone, and her son/husband Oedipus, who did not go into exile but carried on living with his family in Thebes, self-blinded, into old age.[16]

The archetypal mother who dies of grief at the loss of her son is Odysseus's mother, Anticlea, whose ghost he meets in Hades. When she died on Ithaca he was not, as she believed, dead, but he had been away for so long that his parents were giving up hope. A later author, Hyginus, baldly states that she actively killed herself after hearing a false report of Odysseus's death.[17]

Homer's treatment of Anticlea in the *Odyssey* is more ambiguous. In book 11, Odysseus tells the Phaeacians that she was still alive when he left for Troy. She is the second ghost, after his hapless crewman Elpenor, to appear before him in the underworld; at the sight of her he weeps and feels compassion but will not speak to her until he has consulted the prophet Tiresias. When he does allow her to address him, we are told, she wails and asks him how he can have come to the land of the dead if he still lives, and whether he has yet been reunited with Penelope. He tells her that he has not yet returned home, and that he has suffered much, but then he asks what has always struck me as one of the most memorable questions in all Greek literature:

> But come now and tell me this, explaining truthfully.
> What grievous deadly fate overwhelmed you?
> Was it a long illness, or did the archer Artemis
> come for you and kill you with her gentle arrows?

The ancient Greeks believed that some women who died peacefully saw Artemis come to shoot them just before they lost their lives. Odysseus also asks Anticlea what she knows about his father, Laertes, and his wife and son, Penelope and Telemachus.

Anticlea's answer to Odysseus conveys the pain of parents who lose or fear they have lost their children in terms that resonate down the centuries. Laertes is alive, but catatonically depressed. He wears scruffy clothes, sleeps with the slaves in winter and alone in his vineyard in summer,

> lying there in despair, and he nurses his grief in his mind,
> longing for your return, and he has seriously aged.

It was for the same reason that I died and met my fate.
The archer goddess did not find me as a target in my home,
and come against me to kill me with her gentle arrows.
Nor did an illness befall me, the most common cause
of life being driven from sadly wasting limbs.
What robbed me of my honey-sweet life, glorious Odysseus,
was my yearning for you, your advice and your kind-heartedness.

Maybe thoughts of her dead boy child haunted Edith all her remaining life; maybe she imagined what he might have been like as an adult companion; maybe she dreamt of trying to embrace him, only to have him disappear.

Many facets of the complicated Odysseus's character are explored in the *Odyssey,* but kindness is not obvious among them: it is through his dead mother that we first learn he is sometimes capable of this virtue. The pain of their encounter is now exacerbated as he tries three times to embrace her, but she flutters away from him, so his "pain at heart grew ever sharper." I have experienced the same in my dreams, as well as the terrible realization on waking that the mother I had encountered, as Anticlea tells her son, is a mere dreamlike spirit that has long left its flesh and bones.

Edith jumped from an upstairs bedroom window to her death. Jumping is a relatively frequent form of suicide in ancient sources, both historical and fictional. It is one of the three methods, along with hanging and hemlock, that occur as possibilities in a colloquial conversation in Aristophanes' *Frogs.* It is commonly associated with frustrated romantic love: Sappho, Calyce (a chaste maiden who prayed in vain to Aphrodite to make the man she loved marry her, or else she would prefer to die), and many other infatuated characters, both mythical and historical, supposedly leapt from the celebrated Leucadian cliff. This is a steep limestone escarpment on the island now called Lefkada off the western coast of mainland Greece. In Euripides' satyr play *Cyclops*, Silenus says he is prepared to throw himself from the Leucadian rock if only he can procure a drink of wine.

Death by jumping was in ancient sources also often a response to a sudden, unexpected psychological blow. In one of the several versions of her story, Ino had killed her own son Melicertes while temporarily insane, and jumped into the sea with his corpse as soon as she realized what she had done. Aegeus, king of Athens, when he saw his son Theseus's ship returning from Crete with black sails rather than white, assumed that Theseus had been killed by the Minotaur and instantly threw himself, either from the Acropolis or from a clifftop, into the sea. Three Athenian princesses were so terrified at the mere sight of the baby Erichthonios, whose lower half was that of a serpent, that they leapt off the Acropolis.

More apposite to Edith's case is the association of suicide by jumping with an opportunistic impulse—seizing a sudden moment when suicide becomes possible and leaping from a nearby height is quicker and requires less equipment or preparation than death by most other means. Like Sophocles' Ajax, Edith needed to create or seize the opportunity to exit life. Her companion's attention was elsewhere, and she simply climbed onto the window ledge and plunged.

The Greek tragedies that have helped me think about the pain of Edith's existence are two dramas that portray the suicide of an isolated wife and mother responding, directly or indirectly, to an unhappy marriage and absent or deceased children. They are both by Sophocles. In his *Antigone,* Creon, the new tyrant of Thebes, has caused the death by suicide of both his niece Antigone and his son Haemon. Antigone hangs herself rather than die a slow death by starvation when Creon has her walled up in a cave. His son Haemon, who loves Antigone, stabs himself to death beside her corpse. The news is brought to Thebes and relayed to Creon's wife, Haemon's mother, Eurydice. She has not previously been mentioned; Creon is not the kind of man voluntarily to mention in public that he is married. Eurydice clearly has little role in government, unlike her deceased sister-in-law Jocasta in Sophocles' *Oedipus the Tyrant.* Her response to the appalling news is to turn and silently enter the palace.

Creon now appears, carrying the corpse of Haemon, like Lear with the corpse of Cordelia. He is told that Eurydice is also dead. She has stabbed herself to death with a sword. But before doing so she bewailed the death of her other son, "Megareus who died earlier," as well as Haemon's fate. She also cursed Creon, her husband, for causing the deaths of both their sons. Megareus (elsewhere sometimes called Menoeceus) had died in the early hours of the deadly battle at Thebes for an unstated reason that Eurydice blames on her husband. Other sources talk about a voluntary sacrifice to the war god Ares; perhaps he jumped off the city wall. Now a childless widower, Creon is inconsolable. He longs to die himself, although he does not contemplate taking his life. Eurydice did not love her husband, had little to occupy her days, and had lost both her children. But she still had a surviving niece, at least by marriage, Antigone's sister Ismene, who was similarly alone and would have benefited from Eurydice's perseverance in life.

Sophocles' other lonely wife and mother is Deianeira in his *Women of Trachis,* named for its chorus of local women of the town of Trachis, west of Thermopylae. In the play, Heracles has moved his family to the town for safety; they are refugees since he has committed an unabsolved murder. Deianeira opens the play by explaining that she is full of anxiety about her famous husband. She has children with him, but he pays them no attention, merely turning up at sufficient intervals to father another on her: "He looked at them only as the farmer looks at a distant field, visiting it just once to sow seed and once to reap." She is now in "sharp pain" because he has not been seen or heard of for fifteen months;

the Chorus and her old nurse confirm that she is emotionally very low and constantly weeping. She asks her adult son Hyllus for help and he leaves in search of his father.

News soon arrives that Heracles has been victorious in a war in a neighboring region and has sent on ahead some women he has taken captive. There is one who catches Deianeira's eye because she is both beautiful and aristocratic looking. It transpires that Heracles is infatuated with this woman, Iole. He waged the war to gain possession of her as his concubine and, insultingly to Deianeira, has sent her to reside at his marital home.

Deianeira is understandably horrified. Anxious to regain his love, she sends her husband a ceremonial robe to wear as he performs the victory sacrifice, after impregnating it with an ointment she believes to be a love charm that will make him love her alone. But after she has sent the robe, she discovers that the ointment is toxic. She is terrified that she has unwittingly caused his death, and resolves to kill herself if that is the case.

Her son Hyllus, whom she entrusted with the robe, returns, blazing with anger, because the poison is eating into his father's flesh. He speaks to his mother brutally and curses her. She departs the stage, as did Eurydice in *Antigone,* in stunned and ominous silence.

The Chorus hears a scream from inside the house. It is Deianeira's nurse, who has witnessed her mistress's suicide. The nurse enters, and delivers a profoundly touching account of this self-killing. Deianeira had fallen in front of the domestic altars, moaning that there would be nobody to tend them. She touched her household possessions as her tears fell. She wept afresh every time she came across a "well-loved" household slave, and lamented that she would from now on be without her children. Sophocles is stressing repeatedly how many people who lived with and loved Deianeira she was about to leave behind forever. She then climbed onto her marital bed and stabbed herself before the nurse could fetch Hyllus to intervene.

And now Hyllus's agony at his mother's death is given sustained attention. "He knew, poor boy, that he had driven her to do it in his anger." He had now learned that she had not intended to kill Heracles—far from it, she wanted to rekindle her errant husband's love for her.

> And then her wretched son uttered every cry of grief
> as he lamented over her,
> and fell to kiss her on the lips,
> wailing loudly as he lay side by side with her,
> that he had rashly laid a false allegation against her,
> crying that he must now live as an orphan,
> deprived of both his father and of her.

The nurse grimly concludes that there can be no tomorrow for anybody until the day that is present is safely in the past.

Hyllus has yet more trauma to face. His father, even when he learns that Deianeira had acted with the best of intentions, continues to condemn her and expresses no sympathy toward Hyllus for the loss of his mother. He even demands that Hyllus promise to marry Iole, despite Hyllus's horror at the idea. The play ends with the dying Heracles being taken off to be set on fire in a euthanasia on the nearby mountain.

In this tragedy, Heracles is a brutal, insensitive father and husband as well as a mortal. The account of his gentle wife's depression, her despair at discovering that Heracles loves someone else, her silly mistake over the ointment, and her precipitate decision to die are all handled with the greatest delicacy. Hyllus's mistake in showing hatred and aggression toward a woman in this volatile state is clearly delineated. His devastation at losing her could not be described with greater tenderness.

The play holds important lessons for absentee, adulterous, callous husbands, for lonely, neglected women, and for their children. That Sophocles goes out of his way to let us know that Deianeira will also be sorely missed by her household slaves and her other children simply adds to the pathos of this outstandingly painful but illuminating suicide drama.

Congenital depression, boredom, a dead child, the constraints patriarchal bourgeois values imposed on her, as well as an unhappy marriage to a disagreeable husband may all have contributed to Edith's suicidal inclination. She had also been having difficult conversations with my mother. But the literary work that throws most light on the situation is, in her case, perhaps not a Greek tragedy. When I closely examined the beautiful silk picture she had embroidered, I saw a name inscribed upon the urn sitting atop the tomb at which the lady in eighteenth-century costume was mourning. The name is spelt in capital letters: WERTER.

I gasped when I finally recognized the name. It is an anglicized spelling of *WERTHER,* the protagonist of Goethe's *The Sorrows of Young Werther* (1774). This epistolary novel, which culminates in Werther's suicide, was written by Goethe when he was only twenty-four years old, and it turned him into an international literary celebrity almost overnight. It was repeatedly reprinted and translated. Werther's suicide was believed to have inspired a spate of self-killings across Europe. According to Goethe, "My friends . . . thought that they must transform poetry into reality, imitate a novel like this in real life and, in any case, shoot themselves; and what occurred at first among a few took place later among the general public." It was never proven conclusively that Werther's suicide in reality prompted any copycat cases, but the fear of an epidemic was real. Several jurisdictions—Leipzig, Copenhagen, and parts of what was to become Italy—banned the book for a time.[18]

The novel also inspired a variety of fashionable merchandise for decades, especially prints and ceramics featuring Werther's beloved, Charlotte, weeping at his tomb. The embroidery that

Embroidery by Edith Masterton Henderson illustrating Charlotte at Werther's tomb in Goethe's novel *The Sorrows of Young Werther* (1774). (Author's collection, photograph by Richard Poynder, reproduced by permission.)

Edith must have spent months sewing would have been purchased as a painted canvas matched to skeins of appropriately colored silk. The design was based on one such print. Had she identified Charlotte's grief for Werther with her own grief for her father?

Goethe's Werther is a poor but educated middle-class man who wants to be an artist. He leaves home in 1771, and much of the novel consists of his letters to his friend Wilhelm over the twenty months that elapse until his death. In the fictional village of Walheim he falls in love with Charlotte, the daughter of the judge. Her mother has recently died, and she is responsible for her eight younger siblings. She is also betrothed to Albert, a wealthy entrepreneur, who is away, traveling on business. She welcomes the friendship with Werther, and he spends much time with her and the children, becoming obsessed with her.

Realizing that the relationship is doomed, Werther begins to think about suicide, and in order to put a distance between himself and Charlotte he takes a government position at court working for an ambassador. But his egalitarian spirit cannot tolerate the strict class hierarchies inherent in aristocratic society.

Although Charlotte has now married Albert, Werther returns to Walheim. He descends into a depression, exacerbated by regular contact with the woman who only allows expressions of purely platonic love. By November 3, 1772, he is describing his mental state in these terms: "Witness, Heaven, how often I lie down in my bed with a wish, and even a hope, that I may never awaken again. And in the morning, when I open my eyes, I behold the sun once more, and am wretched. If I were whimsical, I might blame the weather, or an acquaintance, or some personal disappointment, for my discontented mind; and then this insupportable load of trouble would not rest entirely upon myself. But, alas! I feel it too sadly. I am alone the cause of my own woe, am I not?" By November 26, he has started reading ancient poets, who help him understand his misery, but he asks, "Have men before me ever been so wretched?"[19]

He begins drinking more heavily and becomes so unhinged that Albert asks Charlotte to stop seeing him. She tells Werther on December 20 that from then on he can visit only by invitation. She does invite him to join them on Christmas Eve. But he ignores her injunction and arrives the next day, when Albert is away on business. She panics, and asks him to read to her from his translation of Ossian—a pseudo-Homeric Celtic Revival epic narrating a heroic death. Charlotte realizes that Werther is planning suicide, and they finally embrace and kiss one another passionately. Horrified at her betrayal of Albert, she locks herself alone in a room. Werther leaves, writes his final letters to her and his friend Wilhelm, and at midnight shoots himself.

The ending of the novel is unbearably bleak. Charlotte passes out with grief when she hears Werther is dead. He had befriended an elderly local man who worked as a steward. These are the final sentences: "The steward and his sons followed the corpse to the grave. Albert was unable to accompany them. Charlotte's life was despaired of. The body was carried by labourers. No priest attended."[20]

Goethe left it to the reader to decide whether Werther's acquaintances were justified in despairing of Charlotte's life. Perhaps my grandmother remained undecided about following her father's suicidal example during the many months she embroidered Charlotte weeping at Werther's tomb, and for many years after. But in the end she wrote the final sentence of her life story in her own blood, leaving my mother with an "illegacy," a burden of grief and anger almost too great to bear.

Chapter 6

THE MOTHER'S TALE

THE GREEK TEXT THAT HAS ILLUMINATED FOR ME what my mother must have gone through after her mother's suicide is Euripides' strange play *Alcestis.* At its center is the voluntary death of a mother, Alcestis, and an agonizing scene in which her husband, but more importantly her children, say good-bye to her. No depiction of a child's reaction to a mother's self-willed death comes close to it in pathos, not even Hyllus's laments over his mother's corpse in Sophocles' *Women of Trachis* that we examined in the previous chapter. Although Alcestis's son and daughter are still children, the scene always comes into my mind when I think about my mother's response to her mother's death because I know she felt bereft of her mother before she was even in her teens. Living with a mother bedridden by depression and unable to pay her little daughter any attention was tantamount to the psychological experience of actual bereavement. Brenda "lost" her mother many decades before that fatal leap from the seaside window.

Alcestis is the wife of Admetus, king of a district in Thessaly, north-central Greece. In a complicated backstory, he has been promised by Apollo that he can postpone his own appointed death if he can find someone prepared to die in his place. His aging parents rather selfishly refuse to do so. Only his wife, Alcestis, volunteers. When the play opens, she is on the point of expiring, we are told, from an unspecified malady, supported inside the palace in the arms of her family. She is much lamented by the chorus of local men, for she has been an exemplary queen as well as wife and mother. The question implicitly arises whether it would not be better for everyone if Admetus dies at his appointed time, avoiding the damage done by Alcestis's voluntary death, rather than assume that he, rather than Alcestis, is somehow indispensable.

The pathos of the situation is enhanced by Alcestis's concern for her children's future after her death. A female servant tells us that Alcestis has prayed at the altar of Hestia, the goddess of the household hearth, asking that both her children find loving spouses and live out long lives in their ancestral land. She returns to her marriage bed, and her little boy and girl cling to her robes in floods of tears as she hugs and kisses them. She says her goodbyes to each of her weeping slaves, however humble.

Admetus now begs her not to die, aware of the grim emotional future the household faces, but it is too late. As Alcestis struggles to stay alive, the Chorus says that the situation is dire enough to make others feel suicidal. Admetus himself, the men say, faces an "unlivable life" from now on. He comes out of the house with his children and ailing wife, who can already see Charon the Ferryman (who ferries dead souls to the underworld) approaching and hear his call; he is followed by the winged figure of Hades himself.

Now, breathing with difficulty, she delivers her instructions to her husband. She prefaces these with the startling information that she knows she had alternatives. If Admetus had died his appointed death, she could have married any Thessalian she wanted "and lived in wealth in a royal house." She loves her life but feels she must place her husband's interests before her own. She reminds him of her altruism in order to put more force into her main request: that he never marry again, because that would put her own children by him at risk from an envious stepmother with power over them. A remarriage would be easier for the boy, she adds, because his father would protect him. But then she turns to her little girl,

> But you, my child, how will your path to womanhood be eased?
> What sort of wife will your father's remarriage impose on you?
> I'm afraid she may spread some malicious gossip about you
> to wreck your chance of marriage when you're in your youthful prime.
> Your own mother will never be beside you to support you
> at your wedding or in childbirth, my child,
> times when nothing is more welcome than a mother's presence.

Alcestis's vision of her little daughter's motherless future is grim. My own mother, Brenda, effectively lost *her* mother's support when she was very young, and her father did little to help either of them. Her mother did attend her wedding, but she was affronted by what she perceived as her own abandonment by her daughter. She certainly was not present when my mother was having her babies. And when Edith eventually took her own life, she left my mother the terrible legacy of psychological pain that the Chorus of *Alcestis* keeps repeating will afflict the house of Admetus forever.

Admetus expresses the agony of any bereaved spouse, whether through voluntary or involuntary death. He promises never to remarry and hopes the children will survive to adulthood. He says he will mourn Alcestis not merely for the conventional period of a year but his whole life. He will never allow banquets, festivities, or music again. He will have a statue made in Alcestis's image to embrace in their bed and hopes she will visit him in dreams. He wishes he had the voice of Orpheus so that he could retrieve her from the underworld, and pleads with her to wait for him there and prepare a postmortem home for them to share after his children bury him in the same coffin by her side.

Alcestis now dies onstage, surrounded by her family and townspeople. In a scene without parallel in ancient or most modern literature, her little son sings a lament full of pain as he embraces her corpse:

> Mother has gone below.
> She exists no longer in the sunlight, father.
> The poor woman has forsaken me and left me motherless for life.
> Look, see her closed eyes and limp arms.
> Listen to me, Mother,
> listen, I implore you.
> It's me, Mother, me, your son,
> Your little one, falling on your lips
> and calling your name.
> . . . .
> Father, I'm young and left to live alone
> deprived of my mother. What cruel things
> I'm suffering, alongside you, my sister.
> O Father, you married her in vain, in vain,
> And have not grown old to die with her.
> She has died before that happened.
> And with your death, Mother,
> the family is devastated.

Instead of a formal, rhetorical obituary, the boy sings straight from the heart, his sentiments raw and simple. For the boy and his sister, the loss of the mother means abject loneliness. The family is indeed devastated.

Admetus takes his dead wife and children into the palace to arrange for the funeral. But first he orders all his subjects to cut their hair short and don black mourning dress. Even the horses' manes are to be shorn. There is to be no instrumental music, leaving unaccompanied the human voice heard in lamentation.

This heartrending scene is of the type which led Aristotle to conclude in his *Poetics* that Euripides was the most tragic of all poets, by which he meant the most effective at producing the appropriate tragic emotions of pity and fear. We desperately pity Alcestis's children and fear that a similar loss might afflict our own family. Yet this odd play now lurches into something more akin to comedy. Admetus's old friend Heracles turns up and miraculously wrests Alcestis from Death, though only after disrupting the funereal atmosphere with boisterous drunkenness.

The seriousness returns in the final scene. Admetus, who does not know that Alcestis has been rescued, despite his promise never to remarry, shockingly accepts the veiled lady Heracles presents to him as a potential bride. He discovers only afterward that she is the resurrected Alcestis. The play has shown us what the voluntary death of a mother does to a family, especially her children, in agonizing detail. And at the end of the play, we are left with the uncomfortable sense that things will never be the same in the house of Admetus. Everyone knows that Admetus accepted his wife's offer, despite knowing what it would do to the children. Everyone has experienced the worst sort of bereavement. And everyone knows that Admetus could not keep his promise to protect his children from the potential threats posed by a stepmother even for a single day. In a sense, despite Alcestis's return, the family is still devastated.

Brenda Henderson remained devastated by her mother's suicide to the end of her own days. Her birth, on September 19, 1925, was a difficult one, necessitating forceps and multiple stitches, as her mother often reminded her. But Edith was delighted with her baby girl. I have seen several photographs taken by fashionable Glaswegian society photographers showing tasteful stagings of cribs and flowing textiles to enhance my grandmother's glamour and my mother's cherubic charm. My mother had some happy memories of her earliest childhood, before my grandmother's depressive periods began to dominate the atmosphere of the household—or at least before my mother became aware of them.

Edith Henderson with her daughter Brenda in 1926. (Author's collection.)

She was taught by a series of governesses and required to appear at meals starting at a young age, formally dressed, to listen to her parents discuss "the state of the nation"; impassive butlers and waiters looked on. Both her parents were liberals and agnostics in the best tradition of David Hume and the Scottish Enlightenment, and Brenda was always well informed about politics. Her parents taught her to read serious articles in the *Times,* attempt the crossword puzzles, and be prepared to analyze what she had read at dinner. She had an enormous vocabulary and was highly articulate, speaking deliberately and with perfect diction in her mild and refined middle-class Scottish lilt.

Recreation, when my grandmother was well, varied. Money was never a problem. My mother learned to swim, dive, and ice skate well and to ride both cross-country and at gymkhanas. Brenda was also given singing lessons and became an excellent Scottish country dancer. But she was always lonely and longed for the company of other children. What she loved best was spending time with her two cousins, her Aunt Ida's children. After Ida married her naval doctor, Maurice Moore, she followed him with their young family to his various postings, which included time spent in Malta. But they would return to Britain for long vacations. The two boys, John and Richard, were slightly younger than Brenda and full of energy and personality. Over long summer vacations she reveled in their company. Photos show them in fancy dress and playing outdoors. They were the brothers she never had and longed for. Her experience of their company was certainly one factor in her later drive to have a large family of her own.

But her mother's depressions became more acute and lasted for longer periods. Walter Henderson's response was to spend ever more hours at his office on Sauchiehall Street, and to involve himself with philanthropic causes. He had little time for his unhappy wife and lonely daughter, but he spent lavishly, encouraging them to go on long vacations without him, to stay with friends or at hotels.

As my grandmother retreated for ever longer periods into the solitary confinement of her bedroom, the blinds drawn, my mother felt increasingly isolated. In her early teens, she begged to go to boarding school to get away from her house of bourgeois misery, and she did attend Harrogate Ladies' College for a single term. She was a plump child and often bullied, and she struggled to make friends. She hated the school and soon returned to Glasgow and her lonely existence in and out of her mother's gloomy bedroom.

When war broke out in 1939, Glasgow life was energized, if for unhappy reasons. Large shipbuilding orders were received on Clydeside. Children from inner-city tenements were evacuated, some arriving at the comparative safety of leafy suburban Pollokshields, only a few miles from their tenement homes. Nocturnal blackouts, strictly enforced, were mightily resented, but nightlife in the more than 100 cinemas, nearly as many theaters, 159 dance halls, and thousands of public houses remained as vigorous as ever.

A furor followed the sinking, south of Rockall, of the SS *Athenia,* a transatlantic liner carrying more than seven hundred people, many of them Jewish, to what they had hoped would be safety in the United States. The vessel had been hit by a German torpedo. Hundreds of survivors were brought to Glasgow, and there was much press interest in the way the local Glaswegian community made them welcome. The American survivors were put up at a hotel on Sauchiehall Street next to my grandfather's law practice. Heavy bombardment in the summer of 1940 brought many fatalities, but nothing on the scale of the Clydeside Blitz of 1941, where as many died in the ensuing fires as in direct hits.

Glasgow suffered terribly in the war, and the massive contribution it made in terms of production of steel and shipbuilding resulted in frequent periods of industrial-relations disputes among its fierce working-class population. My mother and her parents disapproved of such proletarian activism; it was a political point on which she and I were later emphatically to disagree. When victory came, the V.E. celebrations in the center of Glasgow became legendary. Over a hundred thousand people, including my mother and grandmother, gathered in George Square to sing and dance Scottish eightsome reels as the church bells rang. The

City Chambers and university were lit by floodlights for the first time in years. The next morning, three tons of empty bottles had to be removed.[1]

That night was obviously exceptional. But the war had brought not only constant news and excitement, however grim, into my mother's life of suburban genteel captivity; I have inherited a scrapbook containing dozens of newspaper cuttings showing how keenly she followed the progress of the war, especially the public appearances of the royal family and the mobilization and eventual victories of the Soviet army. She loved a joke and inserted a photograph of a white cat with a black mark between his lips and his nose and inscribed the name "Adolf" beneath it. The war also granted her a temporary solution to her personal predicament—what to do with her life. The University of Glasgow encouraged applications even from girls in their mid-teens, since so many seats in lecture halls were empty with all the young men away fighting. My mother continued to live at home, but she enrolled in a degree course in Modern History, specializing in the history of Scotland. Every weekday she took a bus to the university and reveled in the lectures.

She had always enjoyed historical fiction set in Scotland by Walter Scott, Robert Louis Stevenson, James Hogg, and John Galt. Now she discovered Scottish history for real—a passion that never left her. She later took her own children to endless Highland battlefields and spooky castles, and regaled us with tales of doughty rebels against English rule, Robert the Bruce inspired by the spider who would not give up, grim witch hunters, Mary Queen of Scots' lonely incarcerations, and the escapades of gallant Jacobites. She graduated with an upper second degree at the age of nineteen. But what was she to do now?

At some point during the war, letters I have inherited reveal that she had become secretly engaged to John, the older of her Moore cousins, who both trained as general practitioners of medicine. This was in spite of widespread societal disapproval of first cousins marrying each other. She adored both John and his brother and may have met few other candidates for the role of husband. But the young Moores had gone to boarding school in the south; John went on to study medicine at Oxford.[2]

Brenda persuaded her father that she wanted to follow him into the legal profession, although I do not think her heart was in this. She needed to get away from home. Since money was no obstacle, she applied to and was accepted by the University of Oxford to study for a second degree, in law. She loved residing at Saint Hugh's College, and much later became active in the alumnae association. She was never particularly interested in academic legal studies, but once the engagement had become public, she went punting and dancing with her fiancé. She also threw herself into musical activities, both classical music and Scottish folk singing. She became quite sought-after as a reliable, sweet-voiced contralto. Most important, she made her first close friendships with other young women, a couple of which lasted a lifetime. Two of these women became adopted "aunties" to her children, along with our one real aunt, my father's sister Jean. They later talked to me in private much more freely than my mother would about her childhood, aspirations, and family background. Much of the detail in this chapter derives from those conversations.

They told me, for example, that Brenda's mother, Edith, began to show signs of the controlling possessiveness that eventually played a part in her last, suicidal depressions when Brenda left Glasgow for Oxford. Edith was consumed with loneliness, and she moved into a hotel near Saint Hugh's in North Oxford. She came round constantly to visit her daughter and attempted to take over her friendships and social life. It must have been intolerable for a young woman trying to establish her own independence and relationships. When Brenda contracted pneumonia in her second year, Edith was able to take control of her daughter's life entirely.

At this time no antibiotic treatments were available, and it was decided that the damp air of the Thames Valley was no place for a young woman with a serious lung condition. Brenda and Edith spent months in the supposedly more healthful air of Burford, staying at the luxurious Cotswold Gateway Hotel.

Despite her ill health and harassment by her mother, Brenda graduated in law, albeit with an undistinguished degree. She took a job as trainee administrator in the Oxford University Registrar's Office, and was swiftly promoted. As a magnificent organizer, gifted at logistics and planning, she could have had a glittering administrative career. She lived with a friend she had met through her singing, a glamorous and hilarious professional soprano, Marion Milford, who later became my godmother. But Brenda's heart was set on having a family, creating a group of people who loved one another intensely—one obvious response to her miserable parents and lonely childhood.

The engagement to her cousin John did not work out and by 1951 had come to an end. John went on to marry a fellow doctor in 1954. My mother was, I believe, heartbroken, perhaps because for her, this was the loss not just of a fiancé but also of one of her closest relationships from childhood. She never allowed us to ask questions about that time of her life, however. John and Brenda rarely communicated over the following years, although my mother did agree to invite both John and his daughter Barbara to the celebration of her diamond wedding anniversary in Oxford in 2013, and they both attended. When John predeceased her by a couple of years, she was mildly pleased that I went to his funeral but did not go herself.

It was on the rebound that in 1951 she met my father, Stuart Hall, a tall, rather dashing student doing a postgraduate course in theology. He was preparing for ordination in the Church of England. They were introduced at a Scottish Country Dancing Society meeting in Saint Columba's Church off Oxford High

Street. Stuart was not a Scotsman, but he was involved in the band playing the musical accompaniment; my mother sang on those occasions as well as danced. He greatly appreciated my mother's excellent cooking.

My mother now embraced Christianity and was confirmed in the Anglican faith; then, on April 9, 1953, she and Stuart were married in the University Church of Saint Mary the Virgin. They were given the loan of the university car by my mother's boss, the University Registrar, Sir Douglas Veale. All four of their parents attended. But the apparent harmony in the photographs is not remotely true to the strained relationship between Brenda and her parents. Neither approved of the match, for they deeply distrusted all religious people. But social snobbery played a more important role.

Stuart's parents were working class. His father, George Hall, had not been able to cope with working underground in coal mines and had moved to London. By 1953 he was a retired police constable. He had worked with the Met for many years but had never been promoted—he claimed, plausibly enough, because he would not join the Freemasons. He had recently taken up a job as night watchman at a warehouse in Stevenage, one of the ring towns created to absorb overspill from overpopulated poor areas of London under the New Towns Act of 1946. He was taciturn, proud, and funny. As an atheist, in response to a sternly Methodist childhood, he was shocked that his son wanted to go into the church. He was also unimpressed by the Hendersons' status and money.

Stuart's mother, May Hall (née Wale), was a seamstress from an extremely poor family and had no living relatives. All had died in the trenches or in the flu that followed the Great War. She was ambitious for their clever children, both of whom had climbed their way into middle-class circles through scholarships to London grammar schools—opportunities and institutions she had

The wedding of Stuart Hall to Brenda Henderson, April 9, 1953. Walter
Henderson is at the far left, May Hall is fourth from left, Edith Henderson
and Jock Masterton are fourth and third from right, George Hall is at the far
right. (Author's collection.)

enterprisingly researched in the public library. Yet my Scottish
grandparents were not impressed by the seamstress, the security man, and their son, even though he was an Oxford graduate. They wanted Brenda to marry a doctor or a lawyer from a
well-connected family with accumulated capital, not a pious but
impoverished Eastender seeking nothing more high status than
an Anglican curacy.

Brenda and Stuart lived at first in a humble flat in Rose Hill,
Oxford. They were largely estranged at this time from Brenda's
parents. When the following year their first child was born, my
older brother Lindsay, my mother left work. Like her mother
before her, she abandoned any attempt at a career, even though

she was not required to do so. In retrospect I believe this was a huge mistake. She was an extremely competent individual who could have run an entire army, let alone a university. She felt underappreciated and frustrated after dooming herself to continuous domestic drudgery and lacked outlets for her intellect and creativity.

She secured work she could do for money at home by becoming a freelance indexer of academic and middlebrow trade books. She took up several hobbies in addition to singing: golf and gardening in particular. These took her almost nightly out of the house. She became a nationally celebrated teacher of flower arranging. Her recreational activities consumed enough of her time to make me, her third child, resent them bitterly. But with hindsight I can see that they may have been necessary to preserve her mental stability.

The young couple soon moved to Newark, where my father, who had now been ordained, was appointed to a curacy. My sister Nicola was born in 1956. The family then transferred to Edgbaston, Birmingham, where my father taught at Queen's Theological College. I was born in 1959 in the little house on the premises that went with his job. One reason for naming me Edith was to try to please my grandmother, and it worked. She became, to a degree, reconciled with my mother. Regular phone calls and reciprocal visits were reestablished. But my grandmother resented my mother's preoccupation with her husband and three young children. She hated Brenda's nonavailability. She did not include her only child in her will.

In 1959, shortly after I was born, a shocking further suicide within my mother's family hardened her attitudes toward people with a will to self-destruction. Although prone to silent tears, Brenda was otherwise extremely self-controlled and scarcely ever exhibited rage. One of the few occasions when I experienced her irrational anger occurred in early 1993. When my husband-to-be Richard and I first bought a house jointly and moved in together, we settled rather randomly on the East Oxfordshire town of Thame.

It is a pretty market town, with a good state secondary school (we were intending to start a family in due course). But we had no other connection with it or the surrounding area. We had drawn a straight line on a map between my place of work at that time (the University of Reading) and Leicester, then the primary home of Richard's daughter Frances, whom he picked up to spend time with us very regularly. Thame turned out to be more or less on the line we had drawn. We scraped our scanty funds together and jointly bought a modest terraced house that had once been a railway workers' cottage.

But when I rang my mother to tell her where we were moving, she was furious. At the first mention of Thame, she yelled, "How could you?" and slammed the phone down. When I called her back the next day, she was still fuming, but the rage soon turned to tears. On the phone, she demanded to know why I had not remembered "about wicked Cousin Alex." I really had no idea what she meant, and had to press her for information.

Alexander Adam Kidd was my mother's first cousin, but unlike the others in her family who killed themselves, he was in her paternal line. Her father's oldest sister, Sarah Henderson, had married in 1902 and produced two children. One was Alexander, born in 1908 in Glasgow. He had trained as a vet, and by 1933 had become an army captain, serving in the Royal Army Veterinary Force. He married a woman from Buckinghamshire in 1935.

He would have been sent to Doncaster in September 1939 for special training—he was an expert in horses, and there were still two regular and sixteen yeoman cavalry regiments as well as the Life Guards and the Royal Horse Guards to maintain. He seems to have been sent in December 1939 to Haifa via an arduous route: a train journey to Dover, a crossing by sea to Dunkirk, a two-day rail journey to Marseille, and a six-day voyage to Palestine. The horses were suffering from pneumonia, and the men needed to keep a twenty-four-hour patrol in operation. The mobile veterinary unit in which he served was on active service there and in Egypt and Syria, where pack animals and dogs for patrol duties and mine detecting were also used by the army in large numbers. He was later sent to Burma, where conditions for both men and animals were almost indescribably hard. Supplies were chronically short, infestations of insects and vermin were out of control, and contagious diseases were rife. Alex would have seen much suffering. After serving throughout the war, he set up a veterinary practice in Thame. He resided there with his wife at Plough House, 12 Priest's End.[3]

On November 8, 1959, he took his rifle out with him and shot himself through the head. My mother said on the phone that this was in the middle of Thame High Street, by the town hall, although on the family tree she has recorded that it was in the nearby rural district of Ploughley.

The suicide of the well-known local vet, she said, caused an unpleasant and sensational scandal in Thame. The town's population had already endured a disproportionate number of fatalities in the war, and did not like being reminded of those dark times, and in such a lurid manner, by an individual known to almost everyone. My mother did not know why he had done it, although she thought he might have been traumatized during his war service. It is also true, as Émile Durkheim noted, that self-killing has often been treated with less disapprobation in military circles than in most others; medics and vets, too, are statistically more likely to kill themselves than most other types of professionals. Captain Kidd had used a gun which he had acquired on military service and may have used on horses in his veterinary practice. Death by a weapon of war was the model of heroic suicide for ancient military men, notably Ajax, as we have seen. When Antilochus reports to Achilles the death of his beloved Patroclus in the *Iliad*, he grabs the groaning hero's hands for fear he may stab himself in the throat with his blade.[4]

Alex had no children. My mother, living in Birmingham at the time, and therefore one of his few blood relations who was not far away in Scotland, had to go help his widow (coincidentally also called Brenda) arrange his funeral and sort out his effects. Since I was only nine months old, I presume she took me with her.

Thirty-five years later, my mother's fury that Richard and I were living in Thame caused a serious problem in my relationship with her. I was in touch for the first time with the intense rage that the burden of suicide in her family brought on, a white-hot anger smoldering beneath her often impassive, closed-off surface. We stayed in Thame after I moved from a lectureship at Reading to a fellowship at Somerville College, Oxford, in 1995 because it was a much shorter drive to work for me, and we began trying for a baby. Brenda avoided visiting us in Thame, even when we badly needed help at the time of the birth of our younger child in 2000; it felt as though the family curse was fully effective. The Furies were howling for blood. I felt that, just as her mother had been of no help to Brenda as she struggled with the birth of three children within five years, so my mother turned her back on me when I really needed her.

In early 2001, I was afflicted by the third serious depression of my life. Its symptoms were those of postnatal depression, including, for the first and only time in my life, a taste of delusion. I was convinced that our two tiny children were at risk of abduction from some unidentified stranger. This terrifying encounter with the "black dog" did not come immediately following the birth; it was delayed until after the hormonal crash at the end of three years of back-to-back pregnancy and breastfeeding. My husband and a shrewd general practitioner spotted the alarm signals, and I recovered swiftly when put on the correct medication, despite unkind treatment at work from unsympathetic colleagues in the Oxford Classics Faculty. But I became fully reconciled with my mother only after that dark time, some months after we left Thame and moved to Durham in 2001.

She had refused to believe that I genuinely had not known about Wicked Cousin Alex when we decided to move to Thame. It never occurred to her, I suppose, that I might not have chosen to have babies in a town with such a dark familial association when there was no particular reason for moving there. Nor would Richard and I have chosen Thame if I had known how much our living there would upset her. On reflection, I can see that Alex's shocking, violent death, occurring at a time when she was desperately worried about her own mother, would have come as an emotional affront to her. That Alex was on her father's side of the family may also have made her terrified that the depressive tendency was doubly pernicious in her genetic inheritance.

Over the next few years following Alex's death, I think my mother became increasingly afraid that her own mother would follow the example set by both him and her grandfather. She implied to me once that at that time, when she was living in the Midlands with small children and unable to be with Edith, her mother had made threats that Brenda would be sorry if she did not rush whenever required to Edith's side.

Perhaps some suicides have always been associated with attempts to control other people's behavior. Similar coercive threats have been found in private letters written by the Greeks of Roman Egypt, preserved on scraps of papyrus kept dry in the desert sands. The complete psychological picture may be ambiguous: a medical student, for example, tells an elderly priest that unless he communicates with the god Asclepius the young man will do away with himself. Some cases are easier to understand. One desperate woman named Isidora writes to her brother, to whom (according to Egyptian custom) she may have been married, who has been away for two hundred days. He must come home immediately: the baby is extremely ill and thin and may die. "Know with certainty that if it dies in your absence, be prepared lest you find me hanged." Another manipulative death threat, in which the stakes were far less high, was made by a youth called Theon. His father is away in Alexandria and the son writes to him, "If you do not send for me, I'll not eat nor drink either."[5]

Three years after Alex's death, and, I believe, after receiving a number of communications along these lines from her mother, Brenda was devastated by Edith's much-feared suicide. My father told me elliptically that the long drive he took with his weeping wife to Largs, where Edith had finally ended her life, was "rather challenging." The funeral took place in the Largs parish church, the local established Presbyterian Kirk, and my father was asked to contribute a reading. He chose the exceptionally grim Psalm 141, of course in the King James Version of the Bible. Here are its final verses:

> [7]Our bones are scattered at the grave's mouth, as when one cutteth and cleaveth wood upon the earth.
> [8]But mine eyes are unto thee, O GOD the Lord: in thee is my trust; leave not my soul destitute.
> [9]Keep me from the snares which they have laid for me, and the gins of the workers of iniquity.
> [10]Let the wicked fall into their own nets, whilst that I withal escape.

Lord, keep us from the traps, the nets, and snares of destitution and iniquity. Let us who remain survive.

The whereabouts of Edith's grave, if there was one and she was not cremated, are unknown. I have not found it in any Largs cemetery. There was a reception following the suicide, though not in the hotel where it had taken place. Edith's friend Nonie organized everything and played the role of kind and supportive hostess, propping up both Brenda and her father. She also, characteristically, told perhaps inappropriately raucous jokes about men on golf courses committing adultery. I think that was the occasion when my mother decided Nonie was her "real" mother, if an adoptive one. We spent all our school holidays in her house in Elie, Fife, from then on. My mother adored Nonie. The two phoned each other constantly. Non-kin sometimes do far better at love and reciprocal loyalty than those related to us by blood, as Aristotle astutely observed.

But even Nonie's cheery support could not prevent Edith's suicide from inflicting extreme psychological damage on my mother. She became a habitual user of both Valium and Librium. She rarely drank and never smoked, but she overate, especially cheese and creamy desserts, and constantly struggled with her weight. Endless attempts at dieting always culminated in what would now be called binge eating. Her size depressed her further. She wept easily—far too easily as far as I was concerned—every single day. The tears continued to her death; the faintest slight or conflict heralded wet eyes. I learned to tread gingerly around all sensitive topics, suppress my own emotions, keep myself to myself, and be very protective of her.

In the 1960s no real understanding existed of the psychological support needed by the survivors of bereavement by suicide. By the 1980s, however, studies had shown that suicide by a close family member usually results in posttraumatic stress disorder, with symptoms including recurrent recollections of the event, dreams, terror that the whole process is happening again, numbness and a sense of reduced involvement with the world, detachment from relationships, and troubled concentration. Women in particular commonly use tranquilizers to help them cope. What my mother went through with the endless drudgery her three small children inflicted on her (a fourth, Walter, was born in 1965) is difficult to overestimate. She did not, to my knowledge, ever receive therapy or counseling of any kind, although she did sometimes disappear mysteriously for a week or two. I do not know whether this was to visit Nonie or to undergo treatment for anxiety or depression, or both.[6]

I have researched the responses that psychiatrists now identify as the nine main symptoms shown by individuals who have lost a parent to suicide. Most of these ring true to me in the case of my mother when I remember her behavior. There is a tendency toward reality distortion: I do not think my mother ever lied to us about her mother's death, but there was certainly a high degree of evasion and concealment. She was emotionally needy, often demanding displays of affection, with a desperate desire for closeness and yet a fear of it. I know she felt guilty, as if she had caused her mother to kill herself. I don't think she had a disturbed concept of self, but she certainly felt impotent rage at being left to face burdens alone—especially the care of her father, who was eighty years old when his somewhat younger wife died.

I think Brenda relived the suicide frequently. She was privately preoccupied with the topic, while banning discussion of it, and despite seeking comfort in religion did not find it. She tried taking phone calls as a volunteer for the Samaritans, a charity telephone helpline for people contemplating suicide, but found it too upsetting to continue. Her mourning for her mother was disrupted and incomplete; she made no visits to a grave, she did not put photographs of her mother or her own childhood on display, although many existed. She had absorbed society's punitive attitude toward suicide, and told nobody outside the family about it. This psychological situation shaped, through silence and projected anxiety, other family interactions.[7]

In the mid-1980s Nonie died. She fell, broke her hip, and never recovered. My mother was grief-stricken. But her recovery was helped by coming into possession of Nonie's house. She either inherited it, or by the terms of Nonie's will at least had to pay only a very low price for it. Although my father was then employed as

Professor of Ecclesiastical History at King's College London, she packed her bags forthwith (we were then living in the London commuter belt in Saint Albans) and moved north to Elie alone.

My father later took early retirement from academia, accepted the position of parish priest at the Episcopalian (Anglican) church in Elie, and joined her there. But it strikes me as remarkable in hindsight that she was so determined to move north after living in England for forty years. She desperately wanted to be in the sunlit house where she had spent some of the most carefree days of her childhood, and where her mother had been happiest in the company of her beloved friend. As a seaside resort—the third in this family history after Dunbar and Largs—Elie was a perfect place for my siblings and me to take our own children. From the late 1980s until the year before my mother's death in 2016 (with, in my case, a few gaps when we were estranged), Brenda welcomed all four children and all nine grandchildren for holidays. She placed endless conscientiously cooked meals, involving home-grown vegetables and fruit, regularly, three times a day, on the table. She had suffered fearfully on account of the ancestral curse afflicting her family, but she had lived it down and survived.

In later life, in this much-loved house and the garden she turned into a herbaceous paradise, I believe my mother found peace and happiness. She remained permanently tearful, although she stopped taking sedatives. But she would still never talk about her mother, grandfather, or cousin Alex. She had experienced an acute lack of mothering from the time she was a small child. Her mother did not kill herself until my mother was in her late thirties, but that it took so long for the deed to be accomplished in no way diminished the pain my mother suffered. For the bereaved, "The tragedies that hurt the most are those that the sufferers have chosen for themselves."

My mother abhorred the idea of suicide, for understandable personal reasons. But when her own end of life approached, I believe she somewhat foreshortened it by voluntary action. In Roman culture, self-destruction by refusing food, what the Romans called *inedia,* was a death favored by older men, and occasionally women, tired of life. It could be a response to humiliation: when the emperor Caracalla had been deposed and put to death, his mother, Julia Domna, starved herself to death rather than live with her humiliating loss of status. Phaedra in *Hippolytus,* before the secret of her infatuation came out, had first decided to exit life quietly by self-starvation. Even so, inedia was rarely a response to grief. Only the elderly Iphis in Euripides' *Suppliant Women,* after his daughter Evadne kills herself, announces his intention of following her to the grave by refusing food.[8]

My mother did not kill herself, but she arguably shortened her life by refusing food. She was dying of cancer, and she found staying alive in a hospital in Kirkcaldy after a colostomy so unendurable that she ate and drank almost nothing. After losing a great deal of weight, she died in the ward, probably a few weeks prematurely, of sudden kidney failure brought on by dehydration. She was ninety years old. Our relationship had never been easy, and we had sometimes been estranged. But there was never any doubt in my mind that I loved her dearly.

Aristotle distinguishes random memories, which animals including dogs experience, from deliberate, disciplined exercises in recollection, something that as far as we know is a uniquely human capacity. In *Aristotle's Way* I described how I had found that using my own power to recall helped me deal with one especially painful occasion in 2016 at my mother's bedside as she lay dying. Her warm responses—weak hand patting, an occasional smile from between all the tubes—suggest that my recollections helped her as well as me. I consciously set about remembering, in as much detail as possible, moments of great happiness I had felt in her company in my childhood. Old photos and conversations with other members of the family can help prompt memories, but the richest ones are triggered by Aristotle's "deliberate recollection." Systematically paging through my mind the years of my earlier life brought extraordinarily vivid memories flooding back of my mother in her prime. The happiest was of the total delight I had felt as she held me tight as we went down a waterslide in an open-air pool on a summer's day. She managed to mouth through her oxygen mask that she thought this must have been at Dunbar.[9]

Imagine my thrill when in the Dunbar Local History Archive I was not only given a photograph of the old Dunbar Lido, long since demolished, but shown a film of children frolicking there, zooming down the slide, from 1962. As it happens, this is the same year from which my precious memory of blissful union with my mother survives. I think we must have visited Dunbar during the summer my grandmother's suicide was becoming imminent. I was three years old. I can even remember taking the old roll-on-roll-off ferry across the Firth of Forth that was rendered obsolete by the new Forth Road Bridge, which opened in 1964. It was extraordinary to have a blurry, sensual memory of pure filial love visually confirmed in grainy moving images recorded by a cinecamera.

I conclude this chapter with the blog I wrote in 2016, five days after my dauntless mother's death on July 5:

A forlorn week in which my mother died. She was ninety and had been ill for some months. But it has knocked me sideways.

Brenda Mary Henderson Hall was born into a cheerless hautebourgeois Scottish family. An isolated only child, she struggled with her unfeeling father and depressive mother Edith, who eventually committed suicide in the 1960s. But my mother's gutsy response to this early domestic misery was to avoid replicating it at all costs.

This is not to say that one part of her did not remain, for me at least, closed off and mystifying. There were things about her background she flatly refused to discuss. What was admirable was the way she hurled herself into wifehood and motherhood, having four children and nine grandchildren on whom she lavished smiles and delicious meals, always with the fullest-fat ingredients.

She was an old-fashioned Scottish Liberal to the core. She was furious when she appeared in a novel called *The Cellar at the Top of the Stairs* written by an alleged friend of mine. He had modelled its classically educated detective Ethel on his psychedelic impressions of me. He portrayed Ethel's mother as a keen flower arranger (which she was) but also as a supporter of the Conservative Party (which was unthinkable).

Her death has come as I struggle to make the index for an OUP feminist history book I'm co-editing with Rosie Wyles, *Women Classical Scholars: Unsealing the Fountain from the Renaissance to Jacqueline de Romilly*. My mother would have revelled in the subject-matter. I have no idea how to make an index beyond word-searching proper names, and find myself sobbing all over the pdf. She was a world-class professional indexer and is no longer sitting by her computer at the end of the phone. From my first book in 1989 to *Adventures with Iphigenia in Tauris* just two years ago, my mother created brilliant, detailed, thematic, conceptual, intellectually sophisticated and unbelievably useful indexes to almost every book I have published, especially most of the string of collaborative volumes which have come out of the Archive of Performances of Greek & Roman Drama at Oxford.

She was the best indexer of Humanities books ever. She won a National Prize Commendation for the sophisticated research tool which is her index to the enormous *Greek Tragedy and the British Theatre 1660–1914* which I co-authored with Fiona Macintosh in 2005. Mum transformed a monster volume crammed with wildly unfamiliar data into a usable document enhanced by an index of intellectual and aesthetic beauty.

In honour of her I always comment on the quality of indexes in books I review. I hate the mediocrity of the one I'm failing now to compile. She was correct that nobody should index their own books. Like the insightful indexer Claire Minton in Kurt Vonnegut's Hiroshima novel *Cat's Cradle* (1963), she could psychoanalyse any author who indexed their own book just by looking at the concepts they chose to feature.

She was many things to many people, but in adulthood I forged a new collegial bond with her in discussing the minutiae of dating conventions and sub-headings. I doubt if her indexing will feature much in other funeral tributes. So this is my way of saying thanks, mum, and good-bye.[10]

Chapter 7

THE AUTHOR'S TALE

IN ANCIENT RHODES A MAN NAMED TELESPHORUS had offended the tyrant Lysimachus. In reprisal he was kept in a cage, like a wild animal, and fed only unpalatable scraps. A bystander asked why he did not take the dignified way out by ceasing to eat and starving himself to death. Telesphorus simply replied, "A man has everything to hope for while he is still alive": as the Latin source for this story has it, "omnia homini dum vivit speranda sunt." Alongside Aristotle's question—*Whom does suicide injure?*—and the exquisite portraits of both suicidal people and those they leave behind in Greek tragedy, this is one of the principles articulated in ancient sources which kept me from suicide as a young woman. Where there's life, there really is hope.[1]

The ancient Epicureans embraced suicide under certain circumstances, but one of their number, Philodemus, in his *On Death* explicitly advocated caution when deciding that the time to die had arrived. The Greek drama that illustrates this principle perfectly is Sophocles' *Philoctetes.* Even among characters in Greek tragedy, Philoctetes endures far more than his fair share of suffering, and he believes that it is inescapable. The play shows, however, that with the exception of invariably terminal diseases, few horrors faced by humans cannot be remedied or at least ameliorated.[2]

Ten years before the opening of the play's action, Philoctetes was abandoned on the desert island of Lemnos because, through no fault of his own, he had received a snake bite that festered and became gangrenous. His fellow Greeks at Troy could bear neither the smell of the infected wound nor the sound of his screams and so ordered Odysseus to dump him on an island from which he would be unable to escape. As the play opens, Philoctetes has suffered gross loss of status, humiliation at the hands of his former friends and allies, and solitary confinement, forced to subsist on the pitiful diet he has been able to muster by shooting small game. These hardships are compounded by his frequent attacks of unbearable physical pain. But his problem is as much social as physiological. He desperately needs to have his suffering *acknowledged.* The worst aspect of his mental suffering is his fear that nobody except Odysseus and the sons of Atreus is even aware of what he is going through.

It needs to be said that, unlike some more recent cultures, the joy-loving and disarmingly honest ancient Greeks did not believe that suffering ennobled, educated, or improved the character of the sufferer in any sense whatsoever. They thought suffering was terrible, with no redeeming features, and needed to be avoided at all costs. They did not believe that suffering was distributed providentially: they were well aware that good people often suffered, and bad people had been known to die at advanced ages without apparently suffering much at all. As Philoctetes says in reference to the cynical and pitiless Odysseus, "While the gods have apportioned me no enjoyment whatsoever, you are alive and gratified. I endure so much pain and suffering, as well as being mocked by you and the Atridae."

Philoctetes repeatedly expresses degrees of death wish, asking his own personified Life why he has not been allowed to slip down to Hades, or describing his existence as equivalent to being dead. During his first convulsive fit of agony, he begs Neoptolemus (son of Achilles) to cast him into the fires of the volcano on the island and let him burn to death; the volcanic fires also function as an analogy for the pain which surges within Philoctetes' flesh. In his convulsive spasms, he screams for a weapon with which to kill himself, "a sword, or an ax, or any weapon—just get me one!" He wants "to mangle this flesh, to hew limb from limb with my own hand; all I can think of is death." In addition to his suicidal and self-destructive impulses, he is extremely angry about his helplessness; he passes out from pain, and later his bow (which in his maimed state is all that keeps him alive, by enabling him to eat) is removed.[3]

Yet even Philoctetes' apparently insoluble plight can be alleviated. By the end of the play, with the help of his old friend Heracles, who appears to him as a demigod, Philoctetes is persuaded to go with the Greeks back to Troy and be cured by Asclepius's doctor son Machaon. He will have his status as esteemed master of archery restored and play a prominent role in the capture of Troy. But it is the reason why Philoctetes trusts and obeys Heracles that needs to be emphasized. Heracles is a friend—not a blood relative—and bound to him by precious reciprocal ties of loyalty, respect, and promises of protection and aid should the need arise. Even more important, Heracles has suffered a degree—although not the duration—of physical agony equivalent to Philoctetes' own, as the demigod reminds him. Heracles' death was caused by his putting on a garment infused with terrible corrosive poison, which gradually devoured his skin, flesh, and bones. (Heracles' own agony is portrayed in another tragedy by Sophocles I discussed above, *Women of Trachis*.)[4]

Philoctetes knows how terribly Heracles suffered because he was present at the moment Heracles departed mortal existence to become semi-divine. Moreover, he did Heracles the ultimate kindness of putting him out of his misery: he agreed to build a pyre for him on Mount Oeta and set light to it, a deed he recalls proudly to Neoptolemus as having been "the act of a benefactor." Philoctetes, in the world of modern medicine, might have found himself on trial for agreeing to assist Heracles, who was dying a slow and agonizing death, to a swifter demise. But in Sophocles' ethical universe this act of euthanasia for someone facing an inevitable and agonizing death was conceived as doing the sufferer a substantial favor. In the ancient mind, such an act is wholly distinct from the temporary and intermittent urges to self-destruction in a man whose life can potentially be turned around by medical care, concerned friends, restorative social justice, or random good fortune. I wish it could be discussed as a separate phenomenon today.[5]

One more ancient story articulates beautifully the idea that where life is, hope can survive. In this book I have used few Christian narratives, even early ones in ancient Greek, because the prevailing Christian attitude (with exceptions like John Donne's *Biathanatos*) was both censorious, condemning the suicidal individual, *and* lacking in compassion or comfort for those left behind. But one unusual tale in an early Christian novel concerning Saint Peter's ministry manages to be nonjudgmental and compassionate while emphasizing the same principle as that espoused by Telesphorus in his cage: where there is life there is always hope.[6]

Peter encounters a woman who has resorted to begging because her hands are crippled and she cannot work. She tells him that if she were possessed of a sufficiently "manly" spirit, she would throw herself from a height or drown herself to put an end to her misery (these happen to be the methods used by Edith Henderson and Robert Masterton, respectively). Peter, as a conventional Christian, warns her that people who kill themselves may face punishment in the afterlife. The woman responds that she wishes she could believe that souls live on in the underworld.

She tells him her sad story: Her husband went away for a long time, and she was harassed by her lecherous brother-in-law. She escaped by ship with her sons, but they were shipwrecked and she lost contact with them. She stayed on the island of Arados, kept alive by the hope of finding the boys: she would have drowned herself, she says, if she had not held out that hope. When she discovered corpses that she believed were those of her sons, she was saved from suicide by the kindness of neighbors. She was welcomed into their home for as long as she could work with her hands. But a disease that caused "biting pains" (perhaps osteoarthritis) put a stop to that.

The story is framed to emphasize that there is always hope of recovering both happiness and health. She finds one son alive, and her affliction is cured. The point is a Christian one, vindicating Peter's wisdom. But the story is more universal than that, affirming the possibility that circumstances can improve in sudden and surprising ways. This is something that needs to be emphasized in any suicidal crisis.

Because it is not included in the canonical Acts of the Apostles, I did not encounter this story until I was in my thirties, when I was researching the genre of ancient Greek fiction. As so often, this apocryphal apostolic tale provides a fascinating window into the variety in ancient Christian attitudes, even toward suicide; some early church fathers were far kinder and more flexible than the official line taken by the established churches.

My grandmother was not a believer—perhaps an understandable response to the religious conflicts between her father and maternal grandfather. But my mother formally embraced Christianity when she met my father, although I always felt that her religion was little more than skin deep. She rarely attended church when he was absent and did not insist on saying grace before meals or on extended bedtime prayer sessions, as he did. I, on the other hand, was an exceptionally devout child and believed every word of what I was taught. I was convinced that if I were good, God would look after me and I would be rewarded with blissful immortal life in heaven.

At the age of eight I was found weeping by the television watching a report about the starving children in Biafra, where more than a million had died as a result of the three-year Nigerian civil war (1967–70). I do remember asking God why he would let these poor babies suffer when they had done nothing wrong. He did not answer. But then a strange childhood melancholia took hold of me. I started weeping all the time, and refused to get up in the morning to go to school. I found it difficult to accept physical embraces from either parent. My mother was extremely concerned. I overheard her asking my father whether I should be sent to a psychiatrist. He said no. I was, he said, just seeking attention.

Shortly afterward, I was hospitalized for two weeks after an emergency appendectomy. I loved it. The reason was that my mother came on her own to the hospital, without any of my siblings, every single day. I would have her full attention for two whole hours. I did not remember that this had ever happened before, and it certainly never happened subsequently. She did not cry—in fact, she made every effort to cheer me up and read me stories. She brought me cake. It was worth every injection, every painful stitch removal, every pelvic exam.

My own tendency toward tearing up did not find a solution until I left home for university, when my eyes dried up at last. But my teens were turbulent. I have described in *Aristotle's Way* how losing my religion at the age of thirteen left me struggling to figure out moral principles to live by. But at the same time I began to suffer seriously from what has been known (since rather later, the 1990s) as suicidal ideation.

Suicidal ideation is one element of a larger category of mental experience which collectively used to be called "suicidal thoughts." *Ideation* is a word first used by Romantic writers such as Coleridge to mean the creation of mental images. Suicidal ideation is now generally recognized as the first critical step within the suicidal process, though it is not inevitably followed by planning (which also constitutes "suicidal thoughts") or execution of the suicide.

Suicidal ideation, as opposed to actual planning, is now the subject of serious research, and the differences between its prevalence in discrete cultures are being identified. A major World Health Organization study in 2005 produced the startling conclusion that more than a quarter of people interviewed in Durban, South Africa, had experienced suicidal ideation at some point in their lives, whereas in Chennai, India, the proportion was fewer than 3 percent. Yet in Durban, individuals who had experienced suicidal ideation are much *less* likely to kill themselves than individuals in Chennai. A large proportion of people who suffer from suicidal ideation never go on even to plan a suicide attempt, let alone implement the plan. If we were all more open to talking about our psychological experiences, and those of us who often have thoughts about suicide could admit them freely, perhaps the number of completed suicides would drop substantially.[7]

There is one Chorus in Greek tragedy that suffers from suicidal ideation, but acknowledging it seems to *strengthen* the ability of its members to survive adversity. Surprisingly, it is the Chorus of the very tragedy, Aeschylus's *Agamemnon,* that first introduced me in my teens to the fully developed concept of an ancestral curse. The elderly but politically engaged citizens of Argos explore dark emotions in poetry never equaled for emotional force and psychological depth in all Greek drama or, in my estimation, in world literature. In particular, they explore the trauma of a community living in fear of a cruel and tyrannical regime which they struggle to resist, needing to hide their true opinions, and of the brutalizing effect of mass bereavement. But they also survive, as human communities have always survived, whatever the murderous tragedies played out within palace walls and ruling-class families. In their resilience, hope, humanity, and dignity, their skilled acts of recollection, and their insistence on drawing distinctions between what they can and what they cannot control in their communal destiny, these men offer a role model for everyone struggling with psychic pain.[8]

The Chorus's experience is summed up in the famous refrain, occurring four times, "Sing the song of sorrow, but let good prevail." Lament what you have suffered in the past as much as you need, the Chorus urges, but believe that the future may be better. This is a perfect therapeutic mantra in the face of suicidal despair. Oscar Wilde, who had been deeply affected by a performance of *Agamemnon* in Greek in 1880, chose this resonant Greek line as the epitaph to his poem "Tristitiae" (Sorrows). This recommends that, rather than pursuing wealth, the reader should practice respect for the environment and humane sympathy with the hungry and the desolate.[9]

The extensive vocabulary and imagery these old men deploy to express their psychic state are dominated by the emotions of anxiety and terror. But when exploring their inner thoughts, they are almost shockingly honest about their desperation. Three times they even express a death wish, as if they were somehow taking over from the central actors the role of communicating a tragic subjectivity and trying to find relief in psychological candor. They claim that their lives have been made so difficult under the city's current administration that death would have been preferable. One of the Chorus members says, while Agamemnon is being murdered, that it would be far better for them to lose their lives than live under tyranny. After the king's death and Cassandra's the Chorus expresses a longing to meet a swift and painless death in the form of "everlasting sleep."

The community has recently suffered immense war fatalities. "Everyone knows whom they sent off to war, but instead of men, urns and ashes return to the homes of each one." These are dead kinsmen whom the townsmen were never able to lament in person; they could not honor them with the full burial rites so important to every ancient Greek extended family. Their own bereavement keeps triggering flashbacks to their collective trauma the day Iphigenia was slaughtered like a young goat over an altar far away in Aulis. The effect is that of a psychiatric patient on the couch who needs to offload a great burden of remembered trauma before he or she can begin to operate in the real world.

Aeschylus is also insistent that we be conscious of the infirmity of the Chorus, whose members use walking sticks. Advanced age, they sing, "its leaves already withering away, wends its way with three feet, and wanders around, no stronger than a child, like a dream that appears in the daytime." But they know that their acquired practical wisdom, what Aristotle called *phronesis,* gives them authority in old age. These citizens have not lost their moral compass, and in the closing episode they rediscover a spirit of resistance and a physical courage which are inspiring. Aegisthus threatens them: if they do not comply with his tyrannical regime, he will force them to face starvation and imprisonment in darkness. But the old men are defiant: "It would not be the way of the Argives to grovel before an evil man."

So, despite the citizens' misery, which is felt both in the mind and in the body, and makes them envision killing themselves, a sense of resistance and hope can be found in the great choral odes of this drama. I believe these could be used therapeutically to help traumatized individuals explore their pain while committing to survival. We could all benefit from imitating the Argive citizens' principles of emotional honesty, acknowledgment of bereavement, despair, and even suicidal urges, and frustration with the apparent arbitrariness and unfairness of the moral universe. The Argive elders survive, despite the suicidal ideation they have confessed to us, with their dignity and principles intact to wait out the dark times and imagine a better future.

It was in my early teens that I began suffering from suicidal ideation. It commenced at about the time I lost the Christian faith in which I had been raised. It was not, I think, caused by realizing that the Christian taboo on suicide no longer applied to me since I had rejected Christianity. It was more the realization that I found it difficult to adjust to the ramifications of my increasing conviction that our earthly existence is almost certainly our only period of consciousness; even worse was adjusting to the idea that there was neither a providential justice nor a benevolent deity. I lost all belief in life after death, at the same time as I began to be interested in environmental issues and aware that planet earth itself would eventually die. I found myself reading Tennyson's gloomy poem about suicidal former Christians who have become disenchanted with religion:

> Why should we bear with an hour of torture, a moment of pain,
> If every man die for ever, if all his griefs are in vain,
> And the homeless planet at length will be wheel'd thro' the silence of
>   space,
> Motherless evermore of an ever-vanishing race,
> When the worm shall have writhed its last, and its last brother-worm
>   will have fled
> From the dead fossil skull that is left in the rocks of an earth that is
>   dead?[10]

The ideation in my case, which is sporadic but ongoing, usually takes the form of sudden images flashing across my mind's eye. The most common are impulses to jump under moving vehicles, off clifftops, or out of windows. I have been surprised to discover that the images described on August 14, 1944, by Winston Churchill to his doctor, Charles Wilson (1st Baron Moran), almost exactly corresponded with mine: "I don't like standing near the edge of a platform when an express train is passing through. I like to stand right back and if possible get a pillar between me and the train. I don't like to stand by the side of a ship and look down into the water. A second's action would end everything. A few drops of desperation." Images in the other category affecting me portray self-harm with a sharp weapon or a gun. An image of a blade sinking into my forearms appears almost every time I reach for a knife to chop the evening's vegetables. The phenomenon is irritating, exhausting, and distracting. It can erupt inconveniently, interrupting conversations with my family or my concentration on the radio news broadcast. These images increase in number from once or twice a day to hundreds of times a day when I am under stress. At their worst they are accompanied by a buzzing or crackling sound in my ears, like a badly tuned radio. Except briefly in my final year at Oxford, I have never even come close to turning these mental impulses and images into a suicide plan. But until recently I have never felt able to share my experience of them with anyone but my husband.[11]

This is because confessing to suicidal ideation needs careful handling. Many people think suicide is somehow contagious. The ancient Greeks thought so too, and their perception was expressed in the concept of "miasma," physical pollution, which could be spread by physical contact with the corpse of a person who died by suicide or murder, or with the living body or even the gaze of a murderer. Today, the contagion may be conceived as something like a psychological miasma, since incidences of suicide can make suicidal thoughts more likely. Moreover, suicide entails lethal violence, even if it is directed against the self: it would be easy to alarm people on their own behalf as well as mine if they knew what was going on in my mind in upstairs hotel rooms, on railway platforms, or when I opened the kitchen knife drawer.

There can even be unexpected consequences. I was given a mental health checkup form after I had my first baby. It included the question of whether I had ever thought about self-harm and, if so, how often. Since at the time I had not slept for more than two consecutive hours in the six weeks since the birth, I was under significant stress. The rate of suicidal ideations had gone up to at least ten times a day, and I said so. The interviewer was scandalized, and I received a phone call from my general practitioner the same day. I reassured him that suicidal mental images needed to be distinguished sharply from plans for suicide, and the matter was left there. Social Services were not called in. But I had swiftly learned never to admit to experiencing routine suicidal ideation if I could help it.

The only time I did begin to plan a suicide rather than just imagine it was in my final undergraduate year, in 1982. I had not been happy during my first three years of my four-year degree course at Oxford. I was not good at the social side of things within the university community. I utterly failed to collect the address book of contacts with up-and-coming politicians, journalists, entrepreneurs, lawyers, and thespians which so many ambitious Oxford undergraduates hunt down and carry off into their stellar metropolitan lives. My friends were local Oxfordshire people, mostly met through left-wing political activism; despite my Queen's English, inculcated in the elocution classes compulsory for scholarship pupils at Nottingham High School for Girls, I drank in the working-class pubs of Cowley Road.

But I did enjoy my academic work, at least the many hours I spent alone with my Greek texts, displacing the real world from my consciousness and substituting the theaters and philosophical schools of antiquity. I was trying to put Aristotle's secular virtue ethics into practice. Reading his work had convinced me that there was a value in being a good person even in the absence of a providential deity: it might enable me to find an internal source of serenity and to flourish in the long run. Yet the demon of endogenous depression, which I know now was a matter of genetic predisposition, was never far away.

I do not know whether the novelist and poet Stevie Smith was ever diagnosed with endogenous depression. But when I read her autobiographical *Novel on Yellow Paper* in my second undergraduate year, I felt as though I had found a woman with whom I could identify. This extraordinary book, originally published in 1936, was reissued in 1980 by the Virago Modern Classics series, which I, along with thousands of other young feminists, had been following avidly since it was founded in 1978.

It was not just that Smith's fictional alter ego, Pompey Casmilus, had studied ancient Greek in her teens and become obsessed with Greek tragedy, learning whole stretches of Euripides' *Bacchae* off by heart for a school performance; Pompey spends two pages of the novel criticizing Gilbert Murray's overly emotive translation of a speech in Euripides' *Medea* in which the protagonist wonders how it would feel to depart life and find release from pain. It was not just that Pompey/Smith had undergone some kind of mental breakdown at the age of eight, as I had: she had become ill with tubercular peritonitis and was sent away from her mother to a convalescent home. There she spent days on end in tears, hoping to weep herself to death. It was not just that she was constantly worried about her mother's health and had to hide some of her own violent emotions from her. Nor was it that the protagonist/narrator suffers from continuous suicidal ideation— for example, discussing the problem of being unable to find a high enough building in London to jump off to a guaranteed death, whereas in New York it would not be difficult. What really hit home was the passage in which she recommends that all children be taught about suicide to give them strength to conquer fear and *reject* suicide.[12]

For children who are not Christians, she writes, it is important to explain that life may very well at some point feel too painful to bear. They also need to know that they can, at any time, call "Thanatos-Hades the great Lord of the Dead," a figure Alcestis can see coming to take her down to the underworld in Euripides' eponymous play. Armed with this knowledge, such children are far less likely to kill themselves. Life becomes paradoxically bearable if the possibility of a voluntary exit is thought about and embraced. This is a challenging passage, likely to shock many people who abhor the idea of discussing suicide with children. It was probably one of the reasons why the first publisher to whom Smith offered the novel turned it down as too much of a risk. But to me, at the age of twenty-one, it rang unmistakably true.[13]

I realized that I was carrying around with me the possibility that I could leave life at any time if it became any more unbearable. This does not mean I was in danger of doing so. Rather, I had found a mental strategy for enduring the weight of the psychological burden that I felt, most of the time, I was laboring under. To be more precise, the phrase "walking wounded" occurred to me constantly as a description of how I felt while I undertook the tasks that make up the fabric of daily life. This phrase originated in the early twentieth century, coined to classify soldiers who have been casualties of a military conflict but are not considered a medical priority because they can still walk. I don't know why this phrase seemed so apt, since I had not yet discovered that my mother had an uncle (Jock) and a cousin (Alex) whose limbs were intact enough to enable them physically to walk back into Civvy Street at demobilization, yet who never remotely recovered from their experiences of World War I and World War II, respectively.

But there was another aspect of Stevie Smith's responses to Greek tragedy that helped me read its treatment of suicide more sensitively. The playwrights were free, within limits, to alter the traditional myths to create new ethical dilemmas. Euripides seems to have been particularly interested in writing new versions of myths in ways that deleted the suicide of his benighted characters. In his *Phoenician Women,* for example, Jocasta is still alive at an advanced age, living companionably in Thebes with her blinded son/husband Oedipus, having recovered from the shocks she received in Sophocles' *Oedipus the Tyrant.* In Euripides' *Antigone,* which sadly survives only in fragments, Antigone did not kill herself, and neither did Haemon: they married and had a baby. It is almost as if Euripides wanted to show that suicidal impulses were a temporary phenomenon, and that where there's life, there's hope.[14]

Stevie Smith appreciated the flexibility of the Greek tragic myths, and in a hilarious poem she rewrites the story of Phaedra and Hippolytus to suit her own feminist and fun-loving philosophy. She starts not with Euripides but with a revisionist drama, Racine's famous *Phèdre,* in which Hippolytus is not averse to physical relations with women, as in Euripides, but in love with a young woman named Aricie, a rival to Phèdre. Smith wrote her poem "Phèdre" in the early 1960s after watching a production of Racine's tragedy starring the celebrated actress Marie Bell. She proposes a new way of rewriting the story, one in which Theseus conveniently dies, Phèdre and Hippolyte fall in love, and they get married and become respectable. The suicidal heroine would in fact survive, and live down the reputation of her "awful family" and be happy. Smith concludes that classical stories *could* be rewritten: "If I were writing the story / I should have made it a go." The scripts of the future lives of people considering suicide, with proper support, can be rewritten, too.[15]

A friend of mine at the same college killed herself in my first year at Oxford. It was horrifying for the whole community. In my final year I was even more deeply affected by the gruesome suicide of the Classics tutor at Christ Church, Colin MacLeod. I had friends at that college who idolized him. By chance I had sat next to him at a dinner just a couple of weeks before he died; he had been a self-absorbed and astringent conversationalist. But I had made great use of his publications on the tragedian Euripides and the literary critic Longinus and regarded him with awe. He had the kind of job I could then only dream of, he was married, and he was looked up to as a father figure by generations of his students. So why did he drive, in deepest midwinter, to a small local train station, lay his head on the track, and await his death?

All the Oxford Classics undergraduates who had attended his lectures or tutorials were rattled. But I became preoccupied. I discovered that his mentor, Eduard Fraenkel, professor of Latin, had, eleven years earlier, also died by suicide. The possibility that killing oneself might actually be planned and carried out began to prey on my imagination. It could be a tempting reality, I thought, if psychological pain became too great. It was not only possible but demonstrably regarded as a rational choice by people I respected and saw as parental exemplars. The disturbing images of harming myself with which I had been plagued since my early teens, whenever I felt under pressure, gave way to a realization that it might be plausible to act on these frightening impulses.[16]

As the weeks passed and finals approached, I sank into a murky pit of despair. I had worked hard and mastered my set texts, but was exceptionally lonely after a romantic breakup. More important, my waking life was dominated by my desperation to equal the performances of my father and my elder brother, who had both read Classics—then called Literae Humaniores—at Oxford and achieved first class degrees; this was much commented upon and applauded in my hyper-academic family home.

My mother and sister had graduated in other subjects, which the family consensus implicitly deemed intellectually inferior, and had not been awarded firsts. My father was unsympathetic to feminism and had always found it difficult to praise my academic successes. I felt I was bearing the entire history of womankind on my shoulders. Two weeks before the exams started, I realized one morning that I was about to throw myself under a bus on Saint Giles Street. I collapsed in the street, was packed off home, and put under heavy sedation. I returned to take the exams. It was a very hot summer in the Thames Valley, and I drank lager as an anesthetic coolant continuously throughout the long days. I was staggered by the high marks I achieved in the exams (resulting in a first).

My mother's reaction to my depressive episode was terror. During the two weeks I was sedated at home in the run-up to my finals she scarcely left my presence and wept all the time. The ghost of my grandmother sat menacingly between us in the sitting room. But we did not talk at all. I spent that fortnight watching television and rereading, for the twentieth time that year, the most beautiful play about a suicidal crisis in existence, Euripides' *Heracles Mad*, which fortuitously happened to be one of my set texts in my finals. It concludes with an exceptionally moving scene in which a man who has every reason to want to die as soon as possible is persuaded out of taking that irrevocable step by a close friend.

The great hero Heracles appeared often on the Athenian stage, but the depiction of his character varies considerably among plays. Unlike the brutal and insensitive husband and father of Sophocles' *Women of Trachis,* who felt no concern for his children by Deianeira after she had unwittingly caused his imminent death, the Heracles of *Heracles Mad* is an intensely loving family man. He arrives back from his Twelve Labors with obvious delight at his reunion with his elderly human father Amphitryon, who raised him; he fervently greets his wife, Megara, and their three little sons. They have been held captive by Lycus, an evil rival to the Theban throne, in Heracles' absence, and in the first part of the play he has to liberate them from the tyrant. At this climactic point, where happiness should be breaking out for the entire family, he is sent mad on the order of Hera, perennially grudging her stepson (Heracles' biological father was her husband, Zeus) his successes. She sends Lyssa, the semi-canine personification of berserk male violence, half-sister of the Furies, to make him psychotic. Iris, the messenger goddess identified with the rainbow, introduces Lyssa as "the daughter of Night, sprung from the blood of Ouranos" after his castration. In a remarkable speech, we hear how Heracles kills both wife and sons, deludedly imagining them to be the family of his deadly enemy and persecutor, Eurystheus.

Like Sophocles' Ajax, this Heracles has recently attracted sustained attention from scholars who believe both their texts can be used as evidence for the existence of posttraumatic stress disorder in ancient fighting men. Timberlake Wertenbaker's adaptation of Sophocles' play as *Our Ajax*, which premiered at Southwark Playhouse, London, in 2013, incorporated material from interviews she had conducted with former servicemen and their families; they and others were invited to view performances and to participate afterward in public discussions around mental health issues in the military. But *Heracles Mad* also provides a unique document in terms of how to treat a suicidal crisis—without judgment and with offers of support, reassurance that emotional states are temporary, and infinite emotional gentleness.[17]

The last part of the tragedy, as Heracles regains his senses and realizes what he has done, is a masterpiece of sensitive psychology. Heracles is wheeled out of the house onto the stage, providing a terrible tableau; he is bloodied and surrounded by the three little corpses of his children, as the Chorus remarks; the men do not mention his wife, Megara, but her body is probably on the platform alongside them. He had been bound to a pillar to restrain him, and he remains bound, the cords representing the inescapable emotional constraints he must now live under forever.

First his father appears, telling the chorus of old men to restrain their laments in case they wake his sleeping son. He is concerned that Heracles may still be deluded and perform further acts of violence. As Heracles wakes and gradually comes round from his psychotic fit, Amphitryon quietly answers his questions as the poor man pieces together what he has done, asking if he killed Megara as well as his sons. Heracles asks to be released from the bindings, and Amphitryon complies. Heracles sees no alternative but to kill himself immediately:

> Alas! Why should I spare my own life,
> since I've become the murderer of my own most beloved children?
> Why wouldn't I hurry to leap from a steep rock,
> or aim my sword at my guts,
> thus avenging the blood of my sons?
> Or set fire to my flesh, which the goddess sent mad,
> to render my life free of disgrace?

At this critical moment, Heracles' old friend and distant cousin Theseus, king of Athens, a younger man, appears. Heracles had saved him from the underworld, and Theseus explains that they thus have reciprocal obligations toward each other. He decided to come to Thebes when he heard of the abuse of Heracles' family by Lycus, but he now discovers a situation requiring even more urgent action. Heracles sees him approaching and exclaims,

> But look, there's an obstacle to my determination to die—
> Theseus is approaching here, my kinsman and friend.

Heracles is consumed with shame. He fantasizes about flying away, or descending instantaneously to the underworld. He covers his head with his clothes, and says he is terrified that the very sight of him will harm innocent friends. He believes he is physically polluted.

Theseus extracts an account of what has happened from Amphitryon. When Amphitryon explains why Heracles is hiding his face, Theseus, without missing a beat, softly responds, "But I am here to sympathize"—the word is actually stronger, meaning something like "participate in his agony"—"uncover him."

Now Amphitryon utters the kind of speech so many parents of suicidal individuals have uttered, or spoken to themselves, throughout history. He kneels before his inconsolable son, and addresses him:

> O my child, take the clothing off your eyes,
> throw it aside, show your face to the sun.
> Like a weighty wrestling opponent, weeping while I fight,
> I'm holding your beard, your knees, and your hands,
> while the tears fall from my old eyes.
> O my son, control your fierce lionlike temper.
> You're charging toward a bloody and unhallowed show of force.
> What you want is to compound misery with misery.

Heracles may feel that he has no family left, but of course he does. Amphitryon would be heartbroken if Heracles killed himself. But Amphitryon also knows that the suicidal impulse can be a temporary, fleeting state.

Now Theseus speaks up. He also asks Heracles to reveal his face. He reminds him of his own eternal gratitude to Heracles, thus affirming that his friend has done useful things in the past, and produces a new definition of manly excellence: "Noble people bear the calamities sent them by gods and do not refuse them." Where Stoic sages would later see masculine nobility as lying in inevitable suicide if they ever found themselves in Heracles' position, Theseus's radical humanism and perceptive insight into Heracles' own proud personality help him frame the *rejection* of the suicidal escape route as the true mark of a heroic personality.

He unveils his friend, and raises him from his seated position, making him stand and look him in the eye on an equal basis. Theseus is no longer physically talking down to Heracles. This also releases Amphitryon from his suppliant position. The three men stand together to determine the future. Heracles asks why Theseus has unveiled him, and the answer is simple: "You, a mortal, cannot pollute what is of the gods." Heracles has suffered grievously on account of some as yet inexplicable metaphysical force (although Hera is the suspected perpetrator); humans are the creation and the playthings of the gods. Theseus will not allow superstition to dictate how he interacts with the victim these malicious gods had deluded.

Heracles is not convinced; his self-loathing makes him feel that he will damage everything he looks upon. But Theseus insists: the pollution does not pass from one friend to another. This beautiful idea—that love transcends miasma—may have been commonly believed, since in ancient Greece close friends and family needed to handle individuals involved in the taboo-breaking crimes that supposedly incurred pollution. Even Oedipus is allowed to embrace his daughters at the end of *Oedipus the Tyrant.*

Theseus ensures that Heracles knows that he recognizes the scale of the calamity his friend has suffered and repeatedly reassures him that he is wholly sympathetic: "Your miseries reach from earth to heaven"; "I weep for you in the overturning of your fortunes." But since Heracles continues to insist that he will kill himself, Theseus calmly maintains that the truly heroic response to barbarous treatment by the gods is to go on living. Is Heracles' suicide threat, he asks, "indeed the words of Heracles, the muchenduring?" Is suicide appropriate behavior from "humans' benefactor and great friend"? Does Heracles think Greece will take it well if he dies on a perverse impulse? The implicit argument here is that Heracles *is still needed by his wider community.*

And now Theseus *listens.* He listens to Heracles' lengthy monologue detailing the full scope of his tragic predicament and why he finds life unbearable—all fifty-five lines of it. The superhero traces his problems back to his birth: his human father, Amphitryon, had incurred blood guilt before Heracles was born, by accidentally killing Electryon, his uncle and future father-in-law, with a club he had thrown wildly at a disobedient cow. Zeus had caused offense to Hera by fathering him biologically on Amphitryon's wife, Alcmena. The goddess had tried to kill him by putting snakes in his cradle. He had been forced to perform a series of arduous, violent labors. And now he has killed his own wife and children.

As a result of their deaths, Heracles can no longer live in his beloved hometown of Thebes. And everyone will point him out as a disgraced, polluted man. Even the sea and the rivers will refuse to allow him to cross over them. "What right, then, have I to live? What benefit can living a useless and unholy life bestow on me?" But Heracles' attitude is beginning to shift under Theseus's words. He lays the blame firmly at Hera's door and recognizes that he is not only the benefactor of Greece, but effectively "guiltless."

This minor concession allows Theseus the opportunity to put Heracles' own deeds into perspective and, importantly, make an offer of practical help. He points out that other men, too, have encountered terrible tragedy, and even the gods have committed terrible crimes but still live on in Olympus, despite the wrong they have done. So should Heracles.

Theseus then makes the offer that changes everything. It is a plan for an attractive future. He invites Heracles to come with him to Athens, where he will be housed, given lands, and financially supported. When he dies, he will receive sacrifices and a stone memorial. Heracles now sees that it might be more cowardly to die. "The man who cannot withstand catastrophe can never withstand mere weapons. I will persevere in living."

He weeps copiously as he asks Amphitryon to bury the children, their heads resting on their mother's breast, her arms enfolding them. He addresses his deceased wife, Megara, directly, and thanks her for being such a good wife; he says how much he will miss them all. He knows he is still a danger to himself, and asks Theseus to accompany him to Argos, where he needs to deliver the "wretched dog" Cerberus (the last of the Twelve

Labors); he fears that if he travels alone, "sorrow for my sons may damage me."

He now turns to the supportive Chorus, the old men of Thebes, and asks them to give his children burial. Theseus needs to offer Heracles his arm to lean on, and insists that his friend comply, even though Heracles fears he will transfer blood to his friend's clothes. Heracles likens Theseus's behavior toward him to that of a devoted son. They compare notes on times they have felt vulnerable and bereft of all courage: Heracles feels so now, but Theseus admits he had been a coward in Hades.

Heracles addresses his old father. Although Heracles was biologically the son of Zeus, he insists in this play that Amphitryon has played the true father's role—another relationship defined by humane values of reciprocal support rather than a mere blood tie. He promises to come back for Amphitryon and take him to live in Athens once the funerals are accomplished.

The suicidal crisis recedes. Heracles' adoptive father and best friend have seen him through it. They have deployed a combination of nonjudgmentalism, physical support, affirmations of loyalty, acknowledgment of the scale of his suffering, disdain for the superstitious shunning of those involved in violence, expressions of deep sympathy, reminders of how much he is loved and needed, and extensive quiet listening. Theseus knows that he must not leave his friend alone, since he is plainly a danger to himself, and promises to stay close at his side; he also offers a welcome in Athens—a practical solution to Heracles' new predicament as a stateless exile from Thebes.

This is an exemplary handling of a suicidal crisis. It should be read by anyone touched by suicide, suicidal threats, or suicidal impulses. The adoptive father and the loyal friend save Heracles' life. He will live on, bringing benefits to them and to his community: he will "persevere in living." This tragedy's treatment of suicide is profound, humanist, and humane. It also contains a level of psychological sophistication about suicide hardly ever equaled since. It probably saved my life in May 1982. I still reread it often.

Theseus promised Heracles that after his death in Athens he would receive sacrifices and a stone memorial. Heracles was indeed worshipped in Athens, and men swore oaths of friendship to one another in his name. And a stone memorial, an optimistic visual symbol of the possibility of renouncing suicide even in the direst straits, still stands today: it is the Doric temple known as the Theseum, which was actually dedicated to Hephaestus. Heracles' life and labors and his friendship with Theseus were central to the iconography of this building, which was completed shortly before the Parthenon, in the 440s BCE.

With the help of both this startling examination of suicide in Euripides' *Heracles Mad* and medication, I survived my first episode of near-suicide, graduated, and moved on. I took a job of which my parents approved, with a blue-chip shipping company on a management trainee scheme. The interviewers were impressed that I spoke what is rather insultingly to Greeks today called Modern Greek, and thought it might be useful in some of their negotiations. I thought I could convince myself that since the world undoubtedly needs maritime freight transport, I could spend my life usefully organizing it. But I experienced a series of epiphanies which proved to me that I was not cut out for working in the management hierarchy of what I came to see as a profit-driven organization that underpaid and undervalued its ordinary seamen and tugboat operators. I was shocked to discover files detailing the derisory compensation paid to the widows of workers who had lost their lives in the Liverpool docks in the 1950s and 1960s. I left after a year and spent the next twelve months, during 1984–85, working as a volunteer supporting the hungry families of the miners who were on their last great strike against compulsory pit closures.

Increasingly committed to the cause of the poor, I decided, with the help of a wonderful friend and mentor named Margot

Heinemann, that my particular skills and political views would be better deployed in academia, researching classical literature from the perspective of underdogs. My then soon-to-be first husband was studying for a doctorate in philosophy at Oxford, so I signed up for the Classics postgraduate program at the same university to write a thesis on the way ethnic groups are stereotyped in ancient Greek drama. This fitted with my campaigning against apartheid. I felt intellectual stimulation and a sense of purpose. But that is not to say that the demon of endogenous depression never returned to harass me. My second and longer period of acute misery came seven years after my finals crisis.

The direct cause was the despair caused by the deterioration and the break-up of my first marriage. I had spent most of my twenties with the philosopher, but it had become apparent we had irreconcilable differences. I told him the relationship was over on November 9, 1989, emboldened by the sight of East Germans clambering onto the wall that divided Berlin and refusing to accept state coercion and control any longer. What I had not anticipated was the extent of the psychological and physical shock of expelling the primary emotional presence in my life. But Aristotle, good friends, medication, psychotherapy, and my first appointment to a permanent job, at the University of Reading, got me through the crisis.

In therapy I realized that although I passionately wanted to become a mother—far more than I wanted success in the professional arena—I had severe doubts about my ability to be a good enough parent. I had already been through two nervous breakdowns, albeit at moments of great stress and years apart. My grandmother Edith's leap from an upstairs window dominated my visions of motherhood, as did my own mother's incessant weeping. The last thing I wanted was to perpetuate the family curse and encourage the Furies to howl for blood again. Yet after talking for hundreds of hours with an expert psychoanalytical psychotherapist and sticking for seven years with the same tolerant and open-minded boyfriend, I finally realized that I could make as good a go at motherhood as the next woman. And since I have had children, which has brought me far greater joy than anything else in my entire life, suicide has been entirely out of the question. My preoccupation with the ancient Greeks, combined with my experiences with my mother, made me see the suicide of parents almost exclusively from the surviving children's point of view.

I say "almost exclusively." I have also thought about suicide from the parents' perspective. I know several parents who have lost children to suicide, and they never fully recover. It is not only parents, either. The pioneer in this area of psychiatry was once again Edwin Shneidman of the Los Angeles Suicide Prevention Center. He observed as early as 1972 that severe effects can be felt by nonfamily members who interacted regularly with the deceased: roommates, employers, friends, co-workers, teachers, students, physicians, patients. One of the reasons I left my post as tenured university lecturer and classics tutorial fellow at Somerville College in 2001 was that I could not otherwise get beyond the death of a young student in the room next to mine. He was not one of my own charges; he was not studying Classics. But I had been the last person to talk to him the day before his death, when he seemed agitated. He either killed himself deliberately or took an accidental overdose of methadone. The grief of his parents and siblings at the funeral was unbearable. I started shaking every time I entered the college and could not stop.[18]

Professionals in mental health are now increasingly interested in inherited or transgenerational trauma. Particular focus has been laid on the transmission of feelings of pain and loss to the children and more remote descendants of people who have suffered egregiously because they belong to an oppressed community, such as the descendants of slaves in the United States, or of Holocaust victims in Jewish families everywhere, or the brutalized, dispossessed Greeks of Asia Minor and the Black Sea after the 1922 "exchange of populations" with Turkey. But individual trauma can be handed down over generations too.

In 1997, the direct effects on grandchildren of a grandparent dying by suicide were first studied in detail. But Shneidman had already warned that children of suicidal parents needed to take great care not to impose narratives on their own children which assumed they were "just like" a depressive grandparent. Two of Shneidman's colleagues made a case study of a woman whose father died by suicide. She subsequently experienced difficulties with her own young child. She was suffering from emotional depletion as a result of suppressing her own needs, for the demands of the infant made processing the suicide impossible. The relevance of this case to my own and my mother's seems even greater because the woman's problems were exacerbated by being in a bitterly conflicted relationship with her suicidal parent.[19]

A 2012 study of how the bereaved can find a path to recovery notes that children can end up having to be caregivers to parents with a parent who died by suicide. This was certainly the case with my mother, who was forced into the role of her mother's caregiver. Children can also be pushed into strange psychological roles and not allowed to talk about the suicide. "In the worst case such secrets can affect the family for generations." Parents may wish to spare their children the details, but such reticence is not good, since it can make children unable to communicate when they are depressed.[20]

There is no doubt in my mind that my mother projected some of her sadness and anger about *her* mother onto me. This was in spite of—or perhaps a result of—her consistent efforts to protect her children by repressing her own despair and excluding the fact of her mother's suicide from the family conversation. She gave me Edith Masterton's university copy of George Saintsbury's *Loci Critici* when I gave my inaugural lecture as a professor at Durham University in 2002. The card she tucked inside, emblazoned with a photograph of funereal white lilies, reads, "This is a strange and sentimental offering." All my grandparents, she writes, would have been proud of me, "perhaps especially my mother, who had a profound interest in the theatre as well as literature. She greatly valued this book."

The sole nonfinancial legacy my valiant mother left to me in her will is a Victorian bronze statuette of a vaguely Grecian woman cradling a wounded bird. It is a copy of a famous work by the French sculptor Hippolyte François Moreau, who was fashionable across western Europe and the United States in the late nineteenth and early twentieth centuries. It had belonged to my grandmother. My mother told me that woman and bird reminded her of both Ediths. She once said, with tight lips, when I was in a particularly low mood, that we not only were both prone to feeling inappropriate levels of maudlin sympathy for creatures in pain but were wounded in some sense ourselves.

The naming of children needs careful handling. Different cultures reveal different superstitions about using the names of those who died by suicide. Among the Joluo of Kenya, the spirit of a self-killer is felt to be malicious and to constitute a threat to survivors. The custom is for the surviving brother to name his next child after the dead sibling as an act of appeasement and in order to continue the family line. But in ancient Greece, a dream interpreter records that a man who dreamt that he had lost his name ended up hanging himself, with the result that he effectively had no name. The reason is that when living kin conduct their annual festivals for their dead forefathers, they omit from the invitation list the names of those who had killed themselves.[21]

This reminds me of what I think was the systematic destruction of all photographs of my great-grandfather by his wife and children. The fact that a man called Robert Masterton had existed needed erasing. The Joluo and the ancient Greeks knew something about the power of names. My mother was probably

Hippolyte François Moreau, *Jeune fille à la colombe*, bronze copy,
ca. 1870. (Author's collection, photograph by Richard Poynder,
reproduced by permission.)

unwise to call me after a mother she already knew was severely
depressed.[22]

Chapter 8

THE END OF THE JOURNEY: LET GOOD PREVAIL

IN THE FIRST CHAPTER I DESCRIBED MY VIVID EARLY memory of the day in 1962 when my mother heard about her mother's suicide. In July 2022, two months before the 60th anniversary of this event, and a month before the 110th anniversary of Robert Masterton's suicide, I went to Scotland. With my invariably supportive husband Richard Poynder, I had done some preliminary research into censuses, dates, and addresses, and arranged to visit the local archives, where we were helped to discover more.

We did not go to Thame, where our children were born and where my mother's cousin Alex shot himself in 1959. Having lived there for several years in the 1990s and early 2000s, I had long ago identified his home and the rumored sites of his self-destruction. Instead, we headed north across the Scottish border, a car journey I had made innumerable times with my mother over the years.

First we drove to Dunbar and located the large pond where Robert Masterton had been found drowned. It is now a beauty spot. The old quarry has been rewilded. A large variety of birds cluster there, alongside the inevitable crooning seagulls. The vivid Rosebay willowherb was in full bloom. The air was full of the sound of the waves smashing onto the nearby shore, and the smells of gorse and seaweed. I did not realize how close the pond is to the beach, with the Bass Rock and the Island of May, after

Seafield Pond, Dunbar. (Photograph by Richard Poynder, reproduced by permission.)

which Robert's father-in-law had named his boats, visibly jutting out of the Firth of Forth on the northern horizon.

We left the car in the seaside car park, and walked around the pond. I tried to imagine a desperate man in his Edwardian formal clothes wading doggedly toward its center. As a family of ducks swam noisily past, I left a bunch of roses at the water's edge and whispered a greeting to the shade of my great-grandfather, Robert Masterton.

Then we drove into the town and visited the places featuring in my suicidal great-grandfather's and grandmother's daily routine: the High Street where the Mastertons did their shopping and ran what the Scots call general "messages" (errands), the houses they lived in, the town hall with the council room where my great-grandfather had served as burgh chamberlain, the church from which his corpse was carried to its unknown resting place.

A hundred miles west, on the other side of Scotland, lies the spectacular bay of Largs, a charming resort town popular with Glaswegians. Its long, sandy beaches and Victorian promenade nestle beneath the high, heather-clad hills, waterfalls, and misty moorland of the Muirshiel Country Park. Local people still remember the grand old Marine and Curlinghall Hotel; with their help and some old photographs we found the precise spot where limousines used to arrive from Glasgow to deposit well-heeled guests like Edith Henderson to spend their healthful summer vacations. An estate of low-rise apartment blocks has been built in the space where the hotel used to stand, but the far more ancient neolithic stone which stood between it and the sea remains, pointing to the Island of Arran across the wine-dark bay. It seemed an appropriate place for me to leave the pink-and-purple fuchsia I was once told was Edith Masterton's favorite flowering plant.

I felt a curious, almost electrical sensation as I stood within a few yards of the unknown patch of land on which her broken body was found. I thought about my mother receiving the phone call in the hall of her Nottingham family house, and about the little girl sitting on the other side of the drawing-room wall, handling her bricks, listening to her mother bellow.

Last stop was Kirkcaldy. After driving past the hospital where my mother died, we parked at the crematorium where she was cremated in July 2016. Neither I nor my sister Nicky had attended, for reasons still too difficult to air in public, but they had nothing to do with my mother's maternal lineage. We stayed for an hour in the beautifully kept Garden of Memory, and I left a plant, a photo, and a good-bye note.

From the perspective solely of my own psychological health, not attending my mother's funeral rites was a mistake. Her ghost has routinely visited me in nightmarish dreams ever since she died. I am convinced that these apparitions would have been less sad and angry than they have been, at least until recently, if I had been there to watch her coffin disappearing behind the curtains to be lowered into the furnace. This apparition often complains that she has been detained alive somewhere and is only mistakenly believed to be dead. She has begged me to rescue her from wherever she is held captive; rather than see her clearly face to face, often I can only hear her voice from behind a wall or see her dimly through bars or a grubby window.

It was after my crematorium visit that the tears finally came into my eyes, partly for the pain suffered by the dead relatives whose lives' ends I had been tracking on the shores of southern Scotland. But partly they were tears of relief; I felt as if a spiked weight had been lifted from my neck and shoulders. My dream life has subsequently become much calmer; I still receive visits from my mother, but she seems more tranquil as well as more distant now.

I spent the actual sixtieth anniversary of my grandmother's suicide, October 1, 2022, at the joyful wedding of two young colleagues in the center of Edinburgh. The coincidence of the anniversary occurring on the day of the wedding, which I kept to myself, seemed wholly appropriate. And as I write this final chapter on Saint Cecilia's Day, November 22, 2022, I can record that in a dream last week, although she was unaware of me, I heard my mother singing. It was Orfeo's celebrated, melodic aria in act 3 of Gluck's 1752 opera *Orfeo ed Euridice,* "What shall I do without Eurydice?" (Che farò senza Euridice?).

When I was very little Brenda caught me humming it and asked where I had learned it; I had no idea, although she kept the radio on incessantly in our kitchen. (I much resented this when, as an older child, I wanted to have a conversation with her. It was invariably necessary to compete with the BBC Home Service. She hated silence but she did not like talking about personal matters either.) The famous mezzo-soprano Janet Baker's rendition of this aria was much played in the early 1960s; I would have heard the lament either broadcast or performed by my mother herself, who occasionally sang as she did the gardening.

This most recent dream about her was far from nightmarish. It was almost joyous. Although the aria comes at the moment in the opera when Orfeo loses his beloved, the aria my mother was singing in my dream has a surprisingly upbeat melody and, like Handel's "Dead March," is, paradoxically for a funereal song, in the bright, buoyant key of C Major. A nineteenth-century critic, Eduard Hanslick, complained that the brisk, cheery melody sounds far too happy for a lament. But others have responded, I think correctly, that Gluck's music *transcends* Orfeo's grief, translating it into a melodic form that celebrates art's ability to distil despair and sustain human souls.[1]

And when I woke, I realized that my mother's singing had played a crucial role in *her* escape from the ancestral curse. Central to her survival was the model of her uncle Jock, who had persevered in living despite the depressive gene and shellshock. She had also been blessed by her informal "adoptive" mother Aunt Nonie, who had offered her, from her childhood on, simple, conscientious affection, and an example of a woman's life well-lived. But it was through singing that she had forged her first friendships at university, independent of her mother.

Through singing she had met my father. In my childhood she was the contralto star of the productions staged by a Nottingham Gilbert and Sullivan Society; I remember being rather frightened of her as the formidable Dame Carruthers, Housekeeper to the Tower of London in *The Yeomen of the Guard*, and relieved when she wiped off the grease paint at home at the end of the performance. She encouraged all her children to sing and play instruments and diligently drove us to endless music lessons; all four of us have had a lifelong love of music, albeit in very different styles and idioms.

My younger brother Walter read music at university and is a dearly loved teacher of music in a Highland secondary school.

The soundscape of this book has resounded with my mother's laments, Handel's "Dead March," the plangent pipes and sung dirges of Greek tragedy, the cries of seagulls and the roar of the gray sea on breezy Scottish beaches. It is good to replace them here with an inspirational C-Major aria by Gluck and humorous light opera by Gilbert and Sullivan. As I meditate on the role music played in helping my mother unburden herself of the misery imposed on her by familial suicides, I am sitting in the room where I hung the two inherited pieces of needlework, brought from her house a year ago.

I change their position, putting Edith's embroidery of Charlotte grieving at Werther's tomb in a dark, inconspicuous corner. But facing the viewer full-on, by the sunny French windows, on Saint Cecilia's Day 2022 I put my mother's magnificent tapestry of the patron saint of music. Cecilia had sat on her own during her wedding, pouring out her song to the Lord. In my mother's tapestry, she is dressed in elegant medieval costume. She sits confidently at her organ, once again pouring forth delightful music, beneath a canopy of trees. She stares out with a smile on her face directly into the eyes of the viewer; a man and three children accompany her in merry song. The woodland animals scamper, as if hearkening to the music of Orpheus, across the lush green meadow floor.

The journey up my maternal family line has taken me to some bleak scenes and episodes. Squalid living conditions in Victorian factory housing. Lonely deaths by summer seashores. Permanent neurological damage caused on the Somme and personality problems exacerbated by tending sick animals in the Middle East and Burma. Alcoholism, electroconvulsive therapy, and persistent use of Valium. These individual catastrophes have taken place against a historical backdrop that has encompassed vicious schisms in the

Tapestry by Brenda Henderson Hall of Saint Cecilia playing the organ. (Author's collection, photograph by Richard Poynder, reproduced by permission.)

Victorian Church of Scotland; child labor; the temperance movement; women's struggle for the vote, education, and careers; two world wars; the foundation of the National Health Service; the Nigerian civil war; and the fall of the Berlin Wall.

We desperately need better understanding of depression, more encouragement to take suicidal thoughts to a specialist who can support the depressed individual, and proper care of those living with suicidal people or, in the worst case, "postvention" to help those suffering bereavement by suicide. If all these radical changes in society's responses to mental health problems had taken place by the early twentieth century, Robert Masterton and Edith Henderson—and, indeed, Alex Kidd—might not have killed themselves. If they had not killed themselves, my mother, Brenda

Hall née Henderson, would have been spared a huge burden of pain and perhaps found parenting easier.[2]

But the investigation has also revealed achievements and happy moments in the lives of even my most unhappy ancestors. Robert Masterton killed himself in his fifties, but he had lifted himself out of poverty to lead a life of useful service to his community and earn enough money to house his wife and four children handsomely. Jock Masterton conquered alcoholism and shellshock and brought pleasure to thousands as manager of Edinburgh theaters in the 1920s and 1930s. Edith Henderson experienced considerable unhappiness, but she was the first in her family to graduate from a university, laughed long and loud with her sardonic best friend Nonie, and left behind exquisitely embroidered artefacts. My brave mother faced down her ancestral curse. She stared the Furies unleashed by familial bloodshed full in the face and did not give in to them. She had defiantly built her own large family, singing, gardening, and arranging flowers as she did so. She had assembled excellent indexes for many grateful authors, including me, and had always relished expanding her general knowledge in the process. I had discovered a new and profound admiration for her moral courage. And I did not kill myself when I might have done.

The first decades of my life were often disconsolate, but I have spent my later years trying to make the ancient Greeks, whose wisdom on self-killing spoke so loudly to me in my teens and early twenties, accessible to everyone. This book has not been an academic memoir, not even an unconventional one like Kenneth Dover's *Marginal Comment,* which also discusses suicide, albeit from a contrasting perspective; I do hope, however, that I share Dover's candor, which I admire as much as his scholarship. I benefited enormously from his lectures on Greek prose style when I was an undergraduate. This book has not primarily been about me but about the extraordinary scripts dealing with suicide and its consequences for the living, left to us by the Greek tragedians. I hope these plays can find a place in the public and private discussion of suicide.[3]

In his *Ajax*, Sophocles gave us a devastatingly accurate portrait of how a proud military man, when he feels disgraced and abandoned, can use deceit to escape those who love him and kill himself. Euripides' *Alcestis, Hippolytus,* and *Suppliant Women* give voice to the psychological agony of children, spouses, and parents bereaved by a beloved woman's suicide. But in *Agamemnon,* Aeschylus gave us a chorus of old, tired, bereaved ordinary citizens who, despite urges to escape their predicament by suicide, rally to defend themselves against oppression and survive with dignity. Sophocles' *Philoctetes* shows that however hopeless individuals' plights may seem, and however strong their death wish, an improvement in their situation may come suddenly from an unexpected direction. Euripides' *Heracles Mad* gives us extraordinary insight into a dangerous suicidal crisis; in the patient responses of the suicidal man's friend and father to his grief and shame, we possess an invaluable script for helping us think about how to intervene with those seemingly determined to end their own lives.

I also hope that these timeless dramas, along with the story of my own experience of ancestral suicide, have contributed to a secular moral case that can help us, without passing moral judgment on any individuals, to hold despairing loved ones close and dissuade them from voluntary self-destruction. *Sing the song of sorrow, but let good prevail.*

Notes

For the benefit of readers, I have included currently available translations of classical works in the bibliography, but unless otherwise indicated, all translations of classical works are my own. Quotations from the Bible are from the English Standard Version unless otherwise indicated.

Introduction

1. See Hall, *Aristotle's Way,* 4.

2. Quoted in Hecht, *Stay,* 120; Kant, *Groundwork,* 38, 31–32 cited in Hecht, *Stay,* 140–42.

3. Academic studies of suicide in Greek tragedy include Faber, *Suicide and Greek Tragedy;* Loraux, *Tragic Ways of Killing a Woman;* and Garrison, *Groaning Tears.* For studies of biblical narratives, see, e.g., Lowis, *Euthanasia, Suicide, and Despair;* Kaplan and Cantz, *Biblical Psychotherapy.*

ONE. Beginning the Journey

1. The discussions of ancient sources other than Greek tragedy, Plato, and Aristotle in this book are frequently informed by the important collection of data published in van Hooff, *From Autothanasia to Suicide.* An extensive bibliography on suicide in the ancient Greek and Roman worlds can be found in Fögen, "Ars moriendi." See also Aigner, *Selbstmord im Mythos,* and, for a much earlier perspective, Garrisson, *Le Suicide dans l'Antiquité.* My studies include Hall, *Greek Tragedy.*

2. On the play, see further Hall, "Iphigenia and Her Mother at Aulis."

3. On the subject of family curses in general, see Parker, *Miasma,* 191–200, and especially Gagné, *Ancestral Fault in Ancient Greece.*

4. On the Alcmaeonid family, see, e.g., Herodotus, *Histories* 5.71; Thucydides, *History of the Peloponnesian War* 1.126.

5. For discussion of the gendered dimensions of the traditions about the Erinyes, and visual illustrations, see Hall, "Why Are the Erinyes Female?"; on the curse tablet see Wünsch, *Defixionum Tabellae Atticae,* no. 108; the lekythos is Athens, Mus. National 19765, described in Karazou, "An Underworld Scene on a Black-Figured Lekythos."

6. On the Furies as daughters of Night, see Aeschylus, *Eumenides,* l. 416;

as daughters of Darkness, see Sophocles, *Oedipus at Colonus*, l. 40; on their appearance see Junge, *Untersuchungen zur Ikonographie der Erinys*. The fullest account of the Erinyes remains a discussion in Harrison's *Prolegomena to the Study of Greek Religion*, 222–56.

7. See Hall, "Eating Children Is Bad for You."

8. Aristotle, *Nicomachean Ethics* 7.1149b.

9. "Largest Genetic Study of Suicide Attempts."

10. See Moran, *Winston Churchill*, 181; Kim, "The Black Dog Myth." There is no doubt that Churchill suffered from suicidal ideation, on which see Chapter 7, below.

TWO. Who Is Damaged by Suicide?

1. On the film, see Aaron, "Cinema and Suicide," 74–75.

2. See van Hooff, *From Autothanasia to Suicide*, 136–41; Bähr, "Between 'Self-Murder' and 'Suicide,'" 620–32.

3. Confucius, *The Classic of Filial Piety*, in *Analects* 8.3; Job 7:13–19.

4. The dialogue is in Pritchard, *Ancient Near Eastern Texts*, 405–7.

5. See Warren, "Socratic Suicide."

6. Plato, *Phaedo* 116a, 117d.

7. Ibid., 60a, 116b.

8. Ibid., 115b.

9. See Stone, *Trial of Socrates*, 192; Mauthner, *Mrs. Socrates* (in German, *Xanthippe*).

10. The fragment is collected in Valentine Rose, *Aristoteles pseudepigraphus*, frag. 688.

11. The text of Aristotle's will is preserved in Diogenes Laertius, *Lives of Eminent Philosophers* 5.11–16; further quotations are from this text. On Aristotle's final years and will, see Hall, *Aristotle's Way*, 212–14.

12. Aristotle, *Nicomachean Ethics* 5.1138a. Elise P. Garrison discusses the passage in "Attitudes Toward Suicide in Ancient Greece."

13. This injunction is attributed to Aristotle by the proverb compiler Zenobius (6.17).

14. Aristotle, *Nicomachean Ethics* 3.1116a.

15. Aeschines, *Speeches* 3.244; Demosthenes, Oration 57, para. 70.

16. Plutarch, *Life of Theseus* 22.2; Herzog, *Abhandlungen der Preussischen Akademie*, 20–25; see Garrison, "Attitudes Toward Suicide in Ancient Greece," 5–6.

17. Timachidas of Lindos no. 532, in *Die Fragmente der griechischen Historiker*, ed. Felix Jacoby, vol. 3B (Leiden: Brill, 1954) (for a translation,

see Carolyn Higbie, *The Lindian Chronicle and the Greek Creation of Their Past* [Oxford: Oxford University Press, 2003], 47); see Garrison, "Attitudes Toward Suicide in Ancient Greece," 6–7.

18. See Murray, "Plato on Suicide."

19. See Mäkinen, *On Suicide in European Countries,* 13.

20. Pythagoras appears in Cicero's *On Old Age* 20; on Roman practices, see van Hooff, *From Autothanasia to Suicide,* 168.

21. See Chrysippus, paragraph 768, in von Arnim, *Stoicorum Veterum Fragmenta,* 190–92.

22. Epictetus, *Discourses* 1.24.9; Musonius Rufus, *Discourses* 77.7; Pliny the Elder, *Natural History* 2.16, 2.27; Pliny the Younger, *Letters* 1.22.

23. Philodemus, *On Death* 1050, 15.5–6; on Epicurus see Diogenes Laertius, *Lives of Eminent Philosophers* 10.119; the comparison of suicide to leaving a theater is in Cicero, *Academics* 1.15; Lucretius, *The Nature of Things* 3.61.

24. On Lucan see van Hooff, *From Autothanasia to Suicide,* 10; Seneca, *Letters on Ethics* 78.2; Titus Aristo is cited in Pliny the Younger's *Letters* 1.22.8–10; see Mendelson, "Roman Concept of Mental Capacity"; for Agathonice see *The Latin Martyrdom of Carpus, Pamfilus and Agathonice.*

25. Augustine, *City of God* 1.17; Lactantius, *Divine Institutes* 3.18–19; Aquinas, *Summa Theologiae* II part 2, question 64 article 5.

26. More, *Utopia of Sir Thomas More,* 11, 23–27, 223–24, 277; see also Paul D. Green, "Suicide, Martyrdom, and Thomas More."

27. Montaigne, "A Custom of the Island of Cea," in *Essays of Montaigne,* 13. The Valerius Maximus anecdote is in *Memorable Doings and Sayings,* 2.6.

28. Burton, *Anatomy of Melancholy,* 504–5.

29. See Allen, "Donne's Suicides"; Donne, *Biathanatos.*

30. See Allen, "Donne's Suicides," 129; Donne, *Letters to Severall Persons of Honour,* 131–32, 233–34, 268–69, 280–81.

31. Also called *On Suicide.* See Hume, *Life and Correspondence,* 1–45.

32. Hume, *On Suicide,* 1. See also Beauchamp, "An Analysis of Hume's Essay."

33. Edvard Munch, etching and drypoint, *The Suicide* (1896), Munch-Museet, Oslo. Viewable online at https://www.nga.gov/collection/art-object-page.126951. html; see, e.g., ASLEF, The Train Drivers Union, "Trauma Support and Suicide Prevention," https://aslef.org.uk/campaign/trauma-support-and-suicide-prevention.

34. Hume, *Life and Correspondence,* 10; see also 6–7, 143, and Mossner, *Life of David Hume,* 27–28.

35. Rousseau, *Julie*, 321.

36. See Galle, "Sociopsychological Reflections," 559.

37. Diderot, "Suicide"; La Mettrie, *Systeme d'Epicure*, 2:222.

38. See Bricon, *Prud'hon*, 104–21. The painting achieved wide publicity in the form of multiple reproductions of a lithograph by Rose Joseph Lemercie now in the Musée Carnavalet in Paris (https://www.parismuseescollections. paris.fr/en/node/82199#infos-principales).

39. On Chatterton, see Colin Pritchard, *Suicide*, 1–2; Wallis's painting is viewable online at the Tate website: https://www.tate.org.uk/art/artworks/wallis-chatterton-n01685.

40. See Stellino, "Nietzsche on Suicide."

41. On Hecuba, see further Hall, "Trojan Suffering"; Sartre, *Nausea*, 156; Sartre, *Being and Nothingness*, 30.

42. Camus, *Myth of Sisyphus*, 24.

43. James, *Letters of William James*, 38.

44. Cholbi, *Suicide*, 62–63.

THREE. Voices from Greek Tragedy

1. Cutter, *Art and the Wish to Die*, 12; U.K. and U.S. statistics from Bennett, *Suicide Century*, 1; suicide vs. road death statistics in Wertheimer, *A Special Scar*, 4.

2. See, e.g., Minois, *History of Suicide*. On the entry in Johnson's dictionary (London: J. and P. Knapton, 1755) see Barraclough and Shepherd, "Letter to the Editor."

3. On slaves, see *The Digest of Justinian* 21.1, 23.3.

4. Halbwachs, *Causes of Suicide*, 10; Baechler, *Suicides*, 15–20, 319–33, 443–58.

5. Miller, *After the Fall*, 131; Toynbee, *Man's Concern with Death*, 267, 271; for the work of Shneidman, Faberow, and Litman see note 6, below.

6. Shneidman, foreword to Cain, *Survivors of Suicides*, x.

7. See Wertheimer, *A Special Scar*, 8.

8. The earliest text of Plato yet recovered, some early third-century BCE scraps of papyrus found at Arsinoe, is from a copy of the *Phaedo* (P. Petrie i.5–8), proving that the dialogue circulated in Egypt well before Aristophanes' recension. See Turner, *Greek Papyri*, 108. Callimachus's poem, *Palatine Anthology* 7.471, can be found in the Loeb edition of Callimachus and the Loeb translation of *Greek Anthology*, vol. 2; Agathias of Myrine's epigram is in *Greek Anthology* 11.354 (vol. 4 of the Loeb translation). This tradition made Cleombrotus's suicide a popular comic anecdote; see also the Byzantine dialogue *Philopatris* preserved

among Lucian's works, translated in MacLeod, *Lucian,* 414–65.

9. On Hegesius, see Cicero, *Tusculan Disputations* 1.34–36.

10. Hippocrates, *Nature of the Child* 30.11, 82.6–12.

11. Plutarch, *On the Bravery of Women* chap. 11, in *Moralia.*

12. Wertheimer, *A Special Scar,* 87–89; on newspapers and suicide, see Phillips, "The Influence of Suggestion on Suicide."

13. Cain, *Survivors of Suicides,* from *Medical Record* 60 (October 26, 1901): 600–601.

14. See the report of the World Health Organization, *Preventing Suicide,* especially Annex 2, "Overview of the Scientific Literature on the Impacts of Portrayals of Suicide on Stage and Screen," but also Stack, Kral, and Borowski, "Exposure to Suicide Movies," on cinematic suicide.

15. Callimachus, *Epigram* 20.

16. On Phaedra's character see Hall, "Goddesses, a Whore-Wife and a Slave."

17. Thucydides, *History of the Peloponnesian War* 2.46.

18. Bennett, *Suicide Century,* 181.

19. Franzen, "Farther Away"; Adams, Interview with Karen Green.

20. Green, *Bough Down,* 120, 145.

FOUR. The Great-Grandfather's Tale

1. On PTSD, see Wertenbaker, *Our Ajax;* Doerries, "Healing the Invisible Wounds"; on Ajax's suicidal crisis, see the excellent Ph.D. thesis by my former supervisee, Chatterjee, "*Ajax*"; and Seidensticker, "Die Wahl des Todes bei Sophokles."

2. Unless otherwise indicated quotations in this chapter pertaining to the life, death, and funeral service of Robert Masterton are from "Dunbar Burgh Chamberlain Drowned," *Haddingtonshire Courier,* August 16, 1912.

3. "In Memoriam: Robert Masterton," *Haddingtonshire Courier,* August 23, 1912, no page, cutting held in the archives of the John Gray Centre, Haddington, East Lothian.

4. See Humphries, "Childhood and Child Labour."

5. See Laing, *Lecture on the History of Linen;* Laing, *Some Notices of the History of Newburgh.*

6. "Complimentary Gift," *Haddingtonshire Courier,* June 18, 1886.

7. Undated newspaper cutting from unspecified publication in the archives of the John Gray Centre, Haddington, East Lothian.

8. "Parish Council," *Haddingtonshire Courier,* September 27, 1912, n.p., cutting held in the archives of the John Gray Centre, Haddington, East Lothian.

9. "In Memoriam: Robert Masterton."

10. Van Hooff, *From Autothanasia to Suicide,* 141; Seneca, "On Providence" 6.9.

11. See Gates, *Victorian Suicide*; Mallock, *Is Life Worth Living?*

12. "Despair," stanza 11, in Tennyson, *Works of Tennyson,* 226–36; Adams, *A Child of the Age,* 212.

13. See Houston, "The Medicalisation of Suicide," 92.

14. See Turner, *Scottish Secession of 1843*; Henderson, *Heritage.*

15. "The Late Ex-Provost Keir, Dunbar," *Haddingtonshire Courier,* November 14, 1909, no page, cutting held in the archives of the John Gray Centre, Haddington, East Lothian.

16. Chatterjee, "*Ajax.*"

17. The questions about Ajax's burial arise in Philostratus, *Heroicus* 188: "Since the Achaeans were praising Odysseus, Teucer also praised him, but cursed the arms. For, he said, it was not good to bury the cause of death in the same tomb. And they buried him, placing his body in the earth, since Calchas declared that those who kill themselves are not lawfully buried by fire."

FIVE. The Grandmother's Tale

1. Nonnus, *Dionysiaca* 47.214–25, 238–45.

2. "University Cartoons No. 1," *Student,* January 14, 1904, 202–3; A. S. Neill, "Editorial," *Student,* December 4, 1912, 147. On Saintsbury's lecturing style see further Jones, "*King of Critics,*" 199–225.

3. Saintsbury, *Loci Critici,* 425.

4. On Stringer's life and work see Lauriston, *Arthur Stringer.* Stringer's biography of Brooke was *Red Wine of Youth: A Life of Rupert Brooke* (Indianapolis: Bobbs-Merrill, 1948).

5. The hospital and the relationship between Siegfried Sassoon and his psychiatrist during the years Edith was a V.A.D. are at the center of Pat Barker's novel *Regeneration* (1991), which was made into a film of the same name directed by Gillies MacKinnon in 1997.

6. Rose, *Mothers,* 27; Agathias, *Palatine Anthology* 5.97 (collected in vol. 1 of the Loeb *Greek Anthology*).

7. This and much of the subsequent information on Jock Masterton is taken from an interview published on December 31, 1938, in an unknown Scottish newspaper, held as a cutting titled "The Lyceum's Manager Recalls His Early Days" in the archives of the John Gray Centre, Haddington, East Lothian.

8. On PTSD see Shively, et al., "Characterisation of Interface Astroglial Scarring." The information on Jock Masterton in this paragraph is taken from an article published on December 5, 1938, in an unknown Scottish newspaper, held as a cutting in the archives of the John Gray Centre, Haddington, East Lothian, titled "Going to London: Lyceum Theatre Manager Resigning."

9. See Jenkinson, Moss, and Russell, *The Royal*, 277.

10. See Bunch and Barraclough, "The Influence of Parental Death Anniversaries."

11. See Shneidman, "Foreword," in Cain, *Survivors of Suicides*, 6.

12. See van Hooff, *From Autothanasia to Suicide*, 38.

13. See Hippocrates, *Places* 13.19, and *Aphorisms* 2.43; *Asclepiades;* Yapijakis, "Hippocrates of Kos."

14. See Nielsen, *Father-Daughter Relationships*, 264–65.

15. See van Hooff, *From Autothanasia to Suicide*, 26.

16. Barrie, *Peter Pan*, 19. In *Phoenician Women*, Jocasta and Oedipus's daughter Ismene, although her birth is mentioned once, does not otherwise appear.

17. Hyginus, *Fabulae* 243 (in the online text her name is transliterated as both Anticleia and Anticlia).

18. Quoted in William Rose, introduction to J. W. Goethe, *The Sorrows of Young Werther*, trans. Rose (London: Scholastic, 1929), xxiv.

19. Goethe, *The Sorrows of Young Werther*, 322.

20. Ibid., 355.

SIX. The Mother's Tale

1. See Osborne and Armstrong, *Glasgow*, 198–200; Leadbetter, "VE Day in George Square, One Hundred Years On"; and Armstrong, *Glasgow at War, 1939–45*.

2. On the history of their family, see Moore, *Leeches to Lasers*.

3. On the experiences of Alex's army unit, see Clabby, *History of the Royal Army Veterinary Corps*, 118–53.

4. On wartime losses in Thame, see Bretherton and Hickman, *Thame Remembers the Fallen*, 159–220; Durkheim, *Le suicide*, 247; see also Pope, "Concepts and Explanatory Structure in Durkheim's Theory of Suicide"; Platt, "Systematic Review of the Prevalence of Suicide in Veterinary Surgeons"; Bartram, Sinclair, and Baldwin, "Interventions with Potential to Improve the Mental Health and Wellbeing of UK Veterinary Surgeons."

5. Isidora's letter (*PSI* 3.177) is in Bagnall and Cribiore, *Women's Letters from Ancient Egypt;* the priest's and Theon's are in *Oxyrhynchus Papyri* 1.13–14, 1.19.

6. See Lukas and Seiden, *Silent Grief,* 27–42.

7. On common reactions to suicide see Shneidman, "Foreword," in Cain, *Survivors of Suicides,* 6, 13–14, 15.

8. On Julia Domna, see Dio Cassius, *Roman History* 78.23.1; van Hooff, *From Autothanasia to Suicide,* 32.

9. See Hall, *Aristotle's Way,* 220–21.

10. "Goodbye to My Mother the Indexer," July 10, 2016, at https://edithorial. blogspot.com/2016/07/goodbye-to-my-mother-indexer.html?m=0; Stephen Prasher, *The Cellar at the Top of the Stairs* (London: Pan, 1988), 55. Ethel is also sartorially flamboyant, a Fabian and a feminist with a tendency to quote Aristotle. Hall and Macintosh, *Greek Tragedy and the British Theatre.*

SEVEN. The Author's Tale

1. Seneca, *Letters on Ethics: To Lucilius* 70.6–7.

2. Philodemus, *On Death,* P.Herc. 1050, 15.5–6.

3. On this play see Hall, "Ancient Greek Responses to Suffering."

4. For a study of the ethics of *Women of Trachis,* see Hall, "Deianeira Deliberates." For an outstanding analysis of the importance to cultural history of the representation of physical pain in *Philoctetes,* see Budelmann, "The Reception of Sophocles' Representation."

5. On suicide among the sick in antiquity see Gourevitch, "Suicide Among the Sick."

6. The story is found in Clementine, *Apostolical Constitutions* 12, 13/14 = i2.312b–c.

7. See Bertolote et al., "Suicide Attempts, Plans, and Ideation"; Weaver, *Suicidal Ideation,* 5–7.

8. On the Chorus in *Agamemnon,* see Hall, "Sorrow but Survival."

9. Wilde, "Tristitiae," in *Complete Works,* 757.

10. Tennyson, "Despair," stanza 15, in *Works of Tennyson,* 226–36.

11. On Churchill's ideation, see Moran, *Winston Churchill,* 167.

12. Smith, *Novel on Yellow Paper,* 127–29, 155.

13. Ibid., 160–61.

14. For *Antigone,* see Collard and Cropp, *Euripides Fragments,* 156–69.

15. In Smith, "Phèdre," in *Collected Poems,* 426–28.

16. On the suicide, see Mitchell, *Maurice Bowra,* 301; Williams, "Eduard Fraenkel," 442.

17. See Wertenbaker, *Our Ajax.*

18. See Shneidman, "Foreword," in Cain, *Survivors of Suicides,* 16.

19. On grandchildren, see Campbell, "Changing the Legacy of Suicide"; Shneidman, "Foreword," in Cain, *Survivors of Suicides,* 26; the case study is in Augenbraun and Neuringer, "Helping Survivors," 181–83.

20. Dyregrov, Plyhn, and Dieserud, *After the Suicide,* 64, 66.

21. See Artemidorus, *Interpretation of Dreams* 1.4.

22. On naming children after relatives with suicidal impulses, see Bennett, *Suicide Century,* 181–83.

EIGHT. The End of the Journey

1. Hanslick, *On the Musically Beautiful,* 17–18.

2. On postvention see especially Andriessen, "Suicide Bereavement" and Pontiggia et al., "Surviving the Suicide of a Loved One."

3. Dover, *Marginal Comment,* 228–29.

Bibliography

Aaron, Michele. "Cinema and Suicide: Necromanticism, Dead-already-ness, and the Logic of the Vanishing Point." *Cinema Journal* 53 (2014): 71–92.

Adams, Francis William Lauderdale. *A Child of the Age.* London: John Lane, 1894.

Adams, Tim. Interview with Karen Green. *Observer,* April 10, 2011.

Aeschines. *Speeches.* Trans. C. D. Adams. Loeb Classical Library 106. Cambridge: Harvard University Press, 1919.

Aeschylus. *Oresteia: Agamemnon. Libation-Bearers. Eumenides.* Ed. and trans. Alan H. Sommerstein. Loeb Classical Library 146. Cambridge: Harvard University Press, 2009.

Aigner, H. *Der Selbstmord im Mythos. Betrachtungen über die Einstellungen der Griechen zum Phänomen Suizid von der homerischen Zeit bis in das ausgehende 5. Jahrhundert v. Chr.* Vol. 2. Graz: Publikationen des Instituts für Alte Geschichte und Altertumskunde der Karl-Franzens-Universität Graz, 1982.

Allen, Don Cameron. "Donne's Suicides." *Modern Language Notes* 56 (1941): 129–33.

Andriessen, K. "Suicide Bereavement and Postvention in Major Suicidology Journals: Lessons Learned for the Future of Postvention." *Crisis* 35 (2014): 338–48.

Aquinas, Thomas. *The Summa Theologiae of St. Thomas Aquinas.* Rev. ed. London: Benziger Brothers, 1920.

Aristophanes. *Clouds. Wasps. Peace.* Ed. and trans. Jeffrey Henderson. Loeb Classical Library 488. Cambridge: Harvard University Press, 1998.

———. *Frogs.* Trans. Edith Hall. Online text at https://edithhall.co.uk/wp-content/uploads/2023/05/OCR-Frogs.pdf.

———. *Frogs. Assemblywomen. Wealth.* Ed. and trans. Jeffrey Henderson. Loeb Classical Library 180. Cambridge: Harvard University Press, 2002.

Aristotle. *Nicomachean Ethics.* Trans. H. Rackham. Loeb Classical Library 73. Cambridge: Harvard University Press, 1926.

Armstrong, Craig. *Glasgow at War, 1939–45.* Havertown, Pa.: Pen & Sword History, 2019.

Artemidorus. *An Ancient Dream Manual: Artemidorus' The Interpretation of Dreams.* Ed. and trans. Peter Thonemann. Oxford: Oxford University Press, 2020.

Asclepiades, His Life and Writings: A Translation of Cocchi's Life of Asclepiades and Gumpert's Fragments of Asclepiades. Ed. and trans. Robert M. Green. New Haven: Yale University Press, 1955.

Augenbraun, Bernice, and Charles Neuringer. "Helping Survivors with the Impact of a Suicide." In Cain, *Survivors of Suicide,* 178–85.

Augustine. *The City of God.* Trans. William Babcock. Ed. Boniface Ramsey. Hyde Park, N.Y.: New City Press, 2012.

Baechler, Jean. *Suicides.* Trans. Barry Cooper. Oxford: Blackwell, 1979.

Bähr, Andreas. "Between 'Self-Murder' and 'Suicide': The Modern Etymology of Self-Killing." *Journal of Social History* 46 (2013): 620–32.

Barker, Pat. *Regeneration.* London: Viking, 1991.

Barraclough, Brian, and Daphne Shepherd. "Letter to the Editor: A Necessary Neologism: The Origin and Uses of Suicide." *Suicide and Life-Threatening Behavior* 10 (2010): 322.

Barrie, J. M. *Peter Pan: A Fantasy in Five Acts.* London: Samuel French, 1956.

Bartram, D. J., J. Sinclair, and D. S. Baldwin. "Interventions with Potential to Improve the Mental Health and Wellbeing of UK Veterinary Surgeons." *Veterinary Record* 166 (2010): 518–23.

Beauchamp, Tom L. "An Analysis of Hume's Essay 'On Suicide.' " *Review of Metaphysics* 30 (1976): 73–95.

Bennett, Andrew. *Suicide Century.* Cambridge: Cambridge University Press, 2017.

Bertolote, J. M., A. Fleischmann, D. De Leo, J. Bolhari, N. Botega, and D. De Silva. "Suicide Attempts, Plans, and Ideation in Culturally Diverse Sites: The WHO SUPRE-MISS Community Survey." *Psychological Medicine* 35 (2010): 1457–65.

Bretherton, David, and Allan Hickman. *Thame Remembers the Fallen.* Thame, UK: Daal, 2018.

Bricon, Etienne. *Prud'hon: Biographie critique.* Paris: Henri Laurens, 1864.

Budelmann, Felix. "The Reception of Sophocles' Representation of Physical Pain." *American Journal of Philology* 128 (2007): 443–67.

Bunch, J., and B. Barraclough. "The Influence of Parental Death Anniversaries upon Suicide Dates." *British Journal of Psychiatry* 118 (1971): 621–26.

Burton, Robert. *The Anatomy of Melancholy.* Vol. 1. London: George Bell & Sons, 1893.

Cain, Albert C., ed. *Survivors of Suicides.* Foreword by Edwin Shneidman. Springfield, Ill.: Charles C. Thomas, 1972.

Callimachus. *Hecale. Hymns. Epigrams.* Ed. and trans. Dee L. Clayman. Loeb Classical Library 129. Cambridge: Harvard University Press, 2022.

Campbell, F. R. "Changing the Legacy of Suicide." *Suicide and Life-Threatening Behaviour* 27 (1997): 329–38.

Camus, Albert. *The Myth of Sisyphus and Other Essays.* Trans. Justin O'Brien. New York: Vintage, 1991.

Chatterjee, Etta. "*Ajax*—A Study of the Impact and Reception of the Myth of Ajax and Sophocles' *Ajax* in Western Culture." Ph.D. Diss. King's College London, 2019.

Cholbi, Michael. *Suicide: The Philosophical Dimensions.* Peterborough, Ont.: Broadview Press, 2011.

Chrysippus. In *The Hellenistic Philosophers.* Vol. 1: *Translations of the Principal Sources, with Philosophical Commentary.* Trans. A. A. Long and D. N. Sedley. Cambridge: Cambridge University Press, 1987.

Cicero. *On Old Age. On Friendship. On Divination.* Trans. W. A. Falconer. Loeb Classical Library 154. Cambridge: Harvard University Press, 1923.

———. *On the Nature of the Gods. Academics.* Trans. H. Rackham. Loeb Classical Library 268. Cambridge: Harvard University Press, 1933.

———. *Tusculan Disputations.* Trans. J. E. King. Loeb Classical Library 141. Cambridge: Harvard University Press, 1927.

Clabby, J. *The History of the Royal Army Veterinary Corps, 1919–1961.* London: J. A. Allen, 1963.

Clement I. *The Apostolical Constitutions.* Trans. Thomas Smith, Peter Peterson, and James Donaldson. Edinburgh: T. & T. Clark, 1870.

Confucius. *The Analects of Confucius: An Online Teaching Translation.* Trans. Robert Eno. Open Access, 2015. https://chinatxt.sitehost.iu.edu/Analects_of_Confucius_(Eno-2015).pdf.

Cutter, Fred. *Art and the Wish to Die.* Chicago: Nelson-Hall, 1983.

Demosthenes. *Orations.* Vol. 6: *Orations 50–59: Private Cases. In Neaeram.* Trans. A. T. Murray. Loeb Classical Library 351. Cambridge: Harvard University Press, 1939.

Diderot, Denis. "Suicide." In *L'Encyclopédie,* ed. Denis Diderot and Jean Le Rond d'Alembert, 15:639–41. Paris: Briasson, 1751.

Digest of Justinian, The. 4 vols. Translation edited by Alan Watson. Philadelphia: University of Pennsylvania Press, 1998.

Diogenes Laertius. *Lives of Eminent Philosophers.* Vol. 1: *Books 1–5.* Trans. R. D. Hicks. Loeb Classical Library 184. Cambridge: Harvard University Press, 1925.

———. *Lives of Eminent Philosophers.* Vol. 2: *Books 6–10.* Trans. R. D. Hicks. Loeb Classical Library 185. Cambridge: Harvard University Press, 1925.

Doerries, Bryan. "Healing the Invisible Wounds of War with Greek Tragedy." *World Policy Journal* 33 (2016): 54–64.

Donne, John. *Biathanatos.* Ed. Ernest W. Sullivan II. Newark: University of Delaware Press, 1984.

———. *Letters to Severall Persons of Honour.* Ed. Charles Edmund Merrill. New York: Sturgis and Walton, 1910.

Dover, Kenneth. *Marginal Comment: A Memoir.* London: Duckworth, 1994.

Durkheim, Émile. *Le Suicide.* 2nd ed. Paris, 1930.

Dyregrov, Kari, Einar Plyhn, and Gudrun Dieserud. *After the Suicide: Helping the Bereaved to Find a Path from Grief to Recovery.* London: Jessica Kingsley, 2012.

Epictetus. *The Complete Works.* Ed. and trans. Robin Waterfield. Chicago: University of Chicago Press, 2022.

Euripides. *Alcestis, Heracles, Children of Heracles, Cyclops.* Trans. Robin Waterfield. Ed. James Morwood. Introduction by Edith Hall. Oxford. Oxford University Press, 2008.

———. *Bacchae and Other Plays. Iphigenia Among the Taurians, Bacchae, Iphigenia at Aulis, Rhesus.* Trans. James Morwood. Introduction by Edith Hall. Oxford: Oxford University Press, 2000.

———. *Fragments: Aegeus-Meleager.* Ed. and trans. Christopher Collard, Martin Cropp. Loeb Classical Library 504. Cambridge: Harvard University Press, 2008.

———. *Hecuba, The Trojan Women, Andromache.* Ed. and trans. James Morwood. Introduction by Edith Hall. Oxford: Oxford University Press, 2008.

———. *Medea, Hippolytus, Electra, Helen.* Ed. and trans. James Morwood. Introduction by Edith Hall. Oxford: Oxford University Press, 1998.

———. *Orestes and Other Plays. Ion, Orestes, The Phoenician Women, The Suppliant Women.* Trans. Robin Waterfield. Ed. James Morwood. Introduction by Edith Hall. Oxford: Oxford University Press, 2009.

Faber, M. D. *Suicide and Greek Tragedy.* New York: Sphinx, 1970.

Fögen, Thorsten. "Ars moriendi: Literarische Portraits von Selbsttötung bei Plinius dem Jüngeren und Tacitus." *Antike & Abendland* 61 (2015): 21–56.

Franzen, Jonathan. "Farther Away: *Robinson Crusoe,* David Foster Wallace, and the Island of Solitude." *New Yorker* (April 18, 2011): 91.

Gagné, Renaud. *Ancestral Fault in Ancient Greece.* Cambridge: Cambridge University Press, 2013.

Galle, Roland. "Sociopsychological Reflections on Rousseau's Autobiography." Trans. Cathy Waegner. *New Literary History* 17 (1986): 555–71.

Garrison, Elise P. "Attitudes Toward Suicide in Ancient Greece." *Transactions of the American Philological Association* 121 (1991): 1–34.

———. *Groaning Tears: Ethical and Dramatic Aspects of Suicide in Greek Tragedy.* Leiden: Brill, 1995.

Garrisson, Gaston. *Le Suicide dans l'Antiquité et dans les temps modernes.* Paris: Hachette, 1885.

Gates, Barbara. *Victorian Suicide: Mad Crimes and Sad Histories.* Princeton: Princeton University Press, 1988.

Goethe, J. W. *The Sorrows of Young Werther.* In *Novels and Tales by Goethe,* trans. R. D. Boylan, 247–355. London: George Bell and Sons, 1901.

Gourevitch, Danielle. "Suicide Among the Sick in Classical Antiquity." *Bulletin of the History of Medicine* 43 (1969): 501–18.

Greek Anthology, The. Vol. 1. Trans. W. R. Paton. Loeb Classical Library 67. Cambridge: Harvard University Press, 1916.

Greek Anthology, The. Vol. 2. Trans. W. R. Paton. Loeb Classical Library 68. Cambridge: Harvard University Press, 1918.

Greek Anthology, The. Vol. 4. Trans. W. R. Paton. Loeb Classical Library 85. Cambridge: Harvard University Press, 1918.

Green, Karen. *Bough Down.* Los Angeles: Siglio, 2013.

Green, Paul D. "Suicide, Martyrdom, and Thomas More." *Studies in the Renaissance* 19 (1972): 135–55.

Halbwachs, Maurice. *The Causes of Suicide.* Trans. H. Goldblatt. New York: Free Press, 1978.

Hall, Edith. "Ancient Greek Responses to Suffering: Thinking with Philoctetes." In *Human Suffering: Interdisciplinary Perspectives,* ed. Jeff Malpas, 155–69. Dordrecht: Springer, 2011.

———. *Aristotle's Way.* London: Penguin Random House, 2018.

———. "Deianeira Deliberates: Precipitate Decisions in *Trachiniae.*" In *Sophocles and the Greek Tragic Tradition,* ed. Simon Goldhill and Edith Hall, 69–96. Cambridge: Cambridge University Press, 2009.

———. "Eating Children Is Bad for You: Offspring of the Past in Aeschylus' *Agamemnon.*" In *Looking at Agamemnon,* ed. D. Stuttard, 13–27. London: Bloomsbury, 2021.

———. "Goddesses, a Whore-Wife and a Slave: Euripides' *Hippolytus* and Epistemic Injustice Towards Women." In *New Directions in the Study of Women in the Greco-Roman World,* ed. Ronnie Ancona and Georgia Tsouvala, 11–28. Oxford: Oxford University Press, 2021.

———. *Greek Tragedy: Suffering Under the Sun.* Oxford: Oxford University Press, 2010.

———. "Iphigenia and Her Mother at Aulis: A Study in the Revival of a Euripidean Classic." In *Rebel Women: Staging Ancient Greek Drama Today,* ed. John Dillon and S. E. Wilmer, 3–41. London: Methuen, 2005.

———. "Sorrow but Survival: The Therapeutic Moral Example of the Chorus of Aeschylus' *Agamemnon.*" In *He Hennoia tou Ethikou Creous sto Argaio Helleniko Theatro,* ed. Andreas Markantonatos, 52–70. Athens: Foundation for Hellenic Culture, 2022.

———. "Trojan Suffering, Tragic Gods, and Transhistorical Metaphysics." In *Tragedy in Transition,* ed. Sarah Annes Brown and Catherine Silverstone, 16–33. Malden, Mass.: Wiley-Blackwell, 2007.

———. "Why Are the Erinyes Female? or, What Is So Feminine About Revenge?" In *Revenge and Gender in Classical, Medieval and Renaissance Literature,* ed. Lesel Dawson and Fiona McHardy, 33–57. Edinburgh: Edinburgh University Press, 2018.

Hall, Edith, and Fiona Macintosh. *Greek Tragedy and the British Theatre, 1660–1914.* Oxford: Oxford University Press, 2005.

Hanslick, Eduard. *On the Musically Beautiful: A Contribution Towards the Revision of the Aesthetics of Music.* Trans. Geoffrey Payzant. Indianapolis: Hackett, 1986.

Harrison, Jane Ellen. *Prolegomena to the Study of Greek Religion.* Princeton: Princeton University Press, 1991.

Hecht, Jennifer Michael. *Stay: A History of Suicide and the Arguments Against It.* New Haven: Yale University Press, 2013.

Henderson, G. D. *Heritage: A Study of the Disruption.* Edinburgh: Oliver and Boyd, 1943.

Herodotus. *The Histories.* Trans. Aubrey de Sélincourt. London: Penguin, 1954.

Herzog, Rudolf. *Heilige Gesetze von Kos.* Abhandlungen der Preussischen Akademie der Wissenschaften 6. Berlin: Verlag der Akademie der Wissenschaften, 1928.

Hesiod. *Theogony. Works and Days. Testimonia.* Ed. and trans. Glenn W. Most. Loeb Classical Library 57. Cambridge: Harvard University Press, 2018.

Hippocrates. Vol. 1: *Ancient Medicine. Airs, Waters, Places. Epidemics 1 and 3. The Oath. Precepts. Nutriment.* Ed. and trans. Paul Potter. Loeb Classical Library 147. Cambridge: Harvard University Press, 2022.

———. Vol. 4: *Nature of Man. Regimen in Health. Humours. Aphorisms. Regimen 1–3. Dreams. Heracleitus: On the Universe.* Trans. W. H. S. Jones. Loeb Classical Library 150. Cambridge: Harvard University Press, 1931.

———. Vol. 10: *Generation. Nature of the Child. Diseases 4. Nature of Women and Barrenness.* Ed. and trans. Paul Potter. Loeb Classical Library 520. Cambridge: Harvard University Press, 2012.

Homer. *The Iliad.* Trans. Robert Fagles. 2nd ed. London: Penguin, 1992.

———. *The Odyssey.* Trans. Emily Wilson. New York: Norton, 2020.

Houston, Rab. "The Medicalisation of Suicide: Medicine and the Law in Scotland and England, circa. 1750–1850." In *Histories of Suicide: International Perspectives on Self-Destruction in the Modern World,* ed. John Weaver and David Wright, 91–118. Toronto: University of Toronto Press, 2009.

Hume, David. *Life and Correspondence of David Hume.* Vol. 1. Ed. John Hill Burton. Edinburgh: William Tait, 1846.

———. *On Suicide.* London: Penguin, 1905.

Humphries, Jane. "Childhood and Child Labour in the British Industrial Revolution." *Economic History Review* 66 (2013): 395–418.

Hyginus. *Fabulae.* Trans. Mary Grant. Online text at ToposText, https://topostext.org/work/206.

James, William. *The Letters of William James.* Ed. Henry James. London: Longmans, Green, 1926.

Jenkinson, Jacqueline, Michael Moss, and Iain Russell. *The Royal: The History of the Glasgow Royal Infirmary, 1794–1994.* Glasgow: HarperCollins, 1994.

Jones, Dorothy Richardson. *"King of Critics": George Saintsbury, 1845–1933, Critic, Journalist, Historian, Professor.* Ann Arbor: University of Michigan Press, 1992.

Junge, M. *Untersuchungen zur Ikonographie der Erinys in der griechischen Kunst.* Kiel: Christian-Albrechts-Universität, 1983.

Kant, Immanuel. *Groundwork of the Metaphysics of Morals.* Trans. M. Gregor. Cambridge: Cambridge University Press, 1998.

Kaplan, Kalman, and Paul Cantz. *Biblical Psychotherapy: Reclaiming Scriptural Narratives for Positive Psychology and Suicide Prevention.* Lanham, Md.: Lexington, 2017.

Karazou, S. "An Underworld Scene on a Black-Figured Lekythos." *Journal of Hellenic Studies* 92 (1972): 64–73.

Kim, Anna. "The Black Dog Myth: How a Misunderstood Quote Perpetuated the Myth of Churchill's Mental State." Churchill Central, February 26, 2019, https://www.churchillcentral.com/the-black-dog-myth-how-a-misunderstood-quote-perpetuated-the-myth-of-churchills-mental-state/.

Lactantius. *The Divine Institutes, Books 1–7*. Trans. Mary Francis McDonald. Washington, D.C.: Catholic University of America Press, 1964.

Laing, Alexander. *Lecture on the History of Linen and of Linen Manufacture in Newburgh*. Newburgh-on-Tay: James Wood, 1872.

———. *Some Notices of the History of Newburgh*. Newburgh-on-Tay: James Wood, 1871.

La Mettrie, Julien Offray de. *Systeme d'Epicure. L'homme plante. Les animaux plus que machines. Anti-Séneque*. Paris: Charles Tutot, 1796.

"Largest Genetic Study of Suicide Attempts Confirms Genetic Underpinnings That Are Not Driven by Underlying Psychiatric Disorders." Mount Sinai press release, November 29, 2021, https://www.mountsinai.org/about/newsroom/2021/largest-genetic-study-of-suicide-attempts-confirms-genetic-underpinnings-that-are-not-driven-by-underlying-psychiatric-disorders?fbclid=IwAR1VUJ5Uhbs9oUHYOpx1SV9j7WL8MHeTd_00GTFuie4AVcD5LDbNfMpi7fo.

Latin Martyrdom of Carpus, Pamfilus and Agathonice, The. Trans. P. Nowakowski, 2015. Online at https://doi.org/10.25446/oxford.13745173.v1.

Lauriston, Victor. *Arthur Stringer, Son of the North: Biography and Anthology*. Indianapolis: Bobbs-Merrill, 1941.

Leadbetter, Russell. "VE Day in George Square, One Hundred Years On." *Glasgow Times*, May 8, 2015. Online at https://www.glasgowtimes.co.uk/news/13307691.ve-day-in-george-square-one-hundred-years-on/.

Loraux, Nicole. *Tragic Ways of Killing a Woman*. Trans. Anthony Forster. Cambridge: Harvard University Press, 1987.

Lowis, Michael J. *Euthanasia, Suicide, and Despair: Can the Bible Help?: Guidance When Faced with Ethical Dilemmas*. Eugene, Ore.: Wipf & Stock, 2015.

Lucan. *Civil War*. Ed. and trans. S. H. Braund. Oxford: Clarendon, 1992.

Lucretius. *The Nature of Things*. Trans. Alicia Stallings. London: Penguin, 2007.

Lukas, Christopher, and Henry M. Seiden. *Silent Grief: Living in the Wake of Suicide*. Northvale, N.J.: Aronson, 1987.

MacLeod, M. D., trans. *Lucian*. Vol. 8. Loeb Classical Library 432. Cambridge: Harvard University Press, 1967.

Mäkinen, Ilkka Henrik. *On Suicide in European Countries*. Stockholm: Almqvist and Wiksell International, 1997.

Mallock, W. H. *Is Life Worth Living?* London: Chatto and Windus, 1879.

Mauthner, Fritz. *Mrs. Socrates*. Trans. Jacob W. Hartmann. London: Eveleigh Nash & Grayson, 1927.

Mendelson, Danuta. "Roman Concept of Mental Capacity to Make End-of-Life Decisions." *International Journal of Law and Psychiatry* 30 (2010): 201–12.

Miller, Arthur. *After the Fall.* Ed. Brenda Murphy. London: Methuen Drama, 2007.

Minois, Georges. *History of Suicide: Voluntary Death in Western Culture.* Trans. Lydia G. Cochrane. Baltimore: Johns Hopkins University Press, 1999.

Mitchell, Leslie. *Maurice Bowra: A Life.* Oxford: Oxford University Press, 2009.

Montaigne, Michel. *Essays of Montaigne.* Trans. Charles Cotton. Rev. William Carew Hazlitt. Vol. 4. New York: Edwin C. Hill, 1910.

Moore, Richard. *Leeches to Lasers: Sketches of a Medical Family.* Killala, County Mayo, Ireland: Morrigan, 2002.

Moran, Charles. *Winston Churchill: The Struggle for Survival.* London: Constable, 1966.

More, Thomas. *The Utopia of Sir Thomas More in Latin from the Edition of March 1518, and in English from the First Edition of Ralph Robynson's Translation in 1551.* Ed. J. H. Lupton. Oxford: Clarendon, 1895.

Mossner, Ernst Campbell. *The Life of David Hume.* 2nd ed. Oxford: Clarendon, 1980.

Murray, M. "Plato on Suicide." *Phoenix* 55 (2001): 244–58.

Musonius Rufus. *That One Should Disdain Hardships: The Teachings of a Roman Stoic [Discourses].* Trans. Cora E. Lutz. New Haven: Yale University Press, 2020.

Nielsen, Linda. *Father-Daughter Relationships: Contemporary Research and Issues.* London: Routledge, 2012.

Nonnus. *Dionysiaca.* Vol. 3: *Books 36–48.* Trans. W. H. D. Rouse. Loeb Classical Library 346. Cambridge: Harvard University Press, 1940.

Osborne, Brian D., and Ronald Armstrong. *Glasgow: A City at War.* Edinburgh: Birlinn, 2003.

Parker, Robert. *Miasma: Pollution and Purification in Early Greek Religion.* Oxford: Clarendon, 1983.

Phillips, David P. "The Influence of Suggestion on Suicide: Substantive and Theoretical Implications of the Werther Effect." *American Sociological Review* 39 (1974): 340–54.

Philodemus. *On Death.* Ed. and trans. Benjamin Henry. Leiden: Brill, 2010.

Philostratus. *Heroicus. Gymnasticus. Discourses 1 and 2.* Ed. and trans. Jeffrey Rusten and Jason König. Loeb Classical Library 521. Cambridge: Harvard University Press, 2014.

Plato. *The Last Days of Socrates: The Apology, Crito, Phaedo.* Trans. Hugh Tredennick. London: Penguin, 1954.

———. *Laws.* Vol. 2: *Books 7–12.* Trans. R. G. Bury. Loeb Classical Library 192. Cambridge: Harvard University Press, 1926.

Platt, B. "Systematic Review of the Prevalence of Suicide in Veterinary Surgeons." *Occupational Medicine* 60 (2010): 436–46.

Pliny the Elder. *Natural History.* Vol. 1: *Books 1–2.* Trans. H. Rackham. Loeb Classical Library 330. Cambridge: Harvard University Press, 1938.

Pliny the Younger. *Complete Letters.* Ed. and trans. P. G. Walsh. Oxford: Oxford University Press, 2006.

Plutarch. *Lives.* Vol. 1: *Theseus and Romulus. Lycurgus and Numa. Solon and Publicola.* Trans. Bernadotte Perrin. Loeb Classical Library 46. Cambridge: Harvard University Press, 1914.

———. *Moralia.* Vol. 3. Trans. Frank Cole Babbitt. Loeb Classical Library 245. Cambridge: Harvard University Press, 1931.

Pontiggia, M., R. Di Pierro, F. Madeddu, and R. Calati. "Surviving the Suicide of a Loved One: Impact and Postvention." *Recenti progressi in medicina* 112 (2021): 728–41.

Pope, Whitney. "Concepts and Explanatory Structure in Durkheim's Theory of Suicide." *British Journal of Sociology* 26 (1975): 417–34.

Pritchard, Colin. *Suicide—The Ultimate Rejection? A Psycho-social Study.* Buckingham, Pa.: Open University Press, 1995.

Pritchard, J. B. *Ancient Near Eastern Texts Relating to the Old Testament.* Princeton: Princeton University Press, 1950.

Rose, J. *Mothers: An Essay on Love and Cruelty.* London: Faber and Faber, 2018.

Rose, Valentine, ed. *Aristoteles pseudepigraphus.* Leipzig: Teubner, 1863.

Rousseau, Jean-Jacques. *Julie; or, The New Heloise: Letters of Two Lovers Who Live in a Small Town at the Foot of the Alps.* Trans. Philip Stewart and Jean Vaché. In *The Collected Writings of Rousseau,* vol. 6. Hanover, N.H.: Dartmouth College/University Press of New England, 1997.

Saintsbury, George. *Loci Critici.* London: Ginn, 1910.

Sartre, Jean-Paul. *Being and Nothingness: An Essay on Phenomenological Ontology.* Trans. Hazel E. Barnes. Cleveland: Zubal Books, 1982.

———. *Nausea.* Trans. Lloyd Alexander. Norfolk, Conn.: New Directions, 1962.

Seidensticker, B. "Die Wahl des Todes bei Sophokles." In *Sophocle,* ed. Jacqueline de Romilly, 105–44. Entretiens sur l'antiquité classique 29. Vandœuvres-Geneva: Fondation Hardt, 1983.

Seneca. *Letters on Ethics: To Lucilius.* Trans. Margaret Graver and A. A. Long. Chicago: University of Chicago Press, 2015.

———. "On Providence." In *Dialogues and Essays*. Trans. John Davie. Oxford. Oxford University Press, 2007.

Shively, Sharon Baughman, Iren Horkayne-Szakaly, Robert V. Jones, James P. Kelly, Regina Armstrong, and Daniel Perl. "Characterisation of Interface Astroglial Scarring in the Human Brain After Blast Exposure: A Post-mortem Case Series." *Lancet* 15 (2016): 944–53. Online at https://www.thelancet.com/journals/laneur/article/PIIS1474-4422(16)30057-6/fulltext.

Smith, Stevie. *The Collected Poems of Stevie Smith*. London: Allen Lane, 1975.

———. *Novel on Yellow Paper*. London: Virago, 1980.

Sophocles. *Antigone; Oedipus the King; Electra*. Trans. H. D. F. Kitto. Ed. Edith Hall. Oxford: Oxford University Press, 1994.

———. *Oedipus the King. Aias. Philoctetes. Oedipus at Colonus*. Ed. and trans. Oliver Taplin. Oxford: Oxford University Press, 2016.

———. *The Other Four Plays of Sophocles: Ajax, Women of Trachis, Electra, Philoctetes*. Trans. D. R. Slavitt. Baltimore: Johns Hopkins University Press, 2013.

Stack, Steven, Michael Kral, and Teresa Borowski. "Exposure to Suicide Movies and Suicide Attempts: A Research Note." *Sociological Focus* 47 (2014): 61–70.

Stellino, Paolo. "Nietzsche on Suicide." *Nietzsche-Studien* 42 (2013): 151–77.

Stone, I. F. *The Trial of Socrates*. London: Jonathan Cape, 1988.

Tennyson, Alfred. *The Works of Tennyson*. London: Macmillan, 1907.

Thucydides. *History of the Peloponnesian War*. Trans. Rex Warner. London: Penguin, 1954.

Toynbee, Arnold. *Man's Concern with Death*. New York: McGraw-Hill, 1968.

Turner, Alexander. *The Scottish Secession of 1843: Being an Examination of the Principles and Narrative of the Contest Which Led to That Remarkable Event*. Edinburgh: Paton and Ritchie, 1859.

Turner, E. G. *Greek Papyri*. Oxford: Clarendon, 1968.

Valerius Maximus. *Memorable Doings and Sayings*. Vol. 1: *Books 1–5*. Ed. and trans. D. R. Shackleton Bailey. Loeb Classical Library 492. Cambridge: Harvard University Press, 2000.

van Hooff, Anton J. L. *From Autothanasia to Suicide: Self-Killing in Classical Antiquity*. London: Routledge, 1990.

von Arnim, Hans Friedrich. *Stoicorum Veterum Fragmenta*. Vol. 3. Teubner, 1903.

Warren, J. "Socratic Suicide." *Journal of Hellenic Studies* 121 (2001): 91–106.

Weaver, Bradley, ed. *Suicidal Ideation: Predictors, Prevalence, and Prevention*. New York: Nova, 2015.

Wertenbaker, Timberlake. *Our Ajax.* London: Faber, 2013.

Wertheimer, Alison. *A Special Scar: The Experiences of People Bereaved by Suicide.* 2nd ed. London: Routledge, 2014.

Wilde, Oscar. *Complete Works.* London: HarperCollins, 2010.

Williams, Gordon. "Eduard Fraenkel, 1888–1970." *Proceedings of the British Academy* 56 (1970): 415–42.

World Health Organization. *Preventing Suicide: A Resource for Filmmakers and Others Working on Stage and Screen,* 2019. Online at https://www.who.int/publications/i/item/preventing-suicide-a-resource-for-filmmakers-and-others-working-on-stage-and-screen.

Wünsch, Richard, ed. *Defixionum Tabellae Atticae.* Berlin: Georg Reimer, 1897.

Xenophon. *Memorabilia.* Trans. Amy L. Bonnette. Ithaca: Cornell University Press, 1994.

Yapijakis, Christos. "Hippocrates of Kos, the Father of Clinical Medicine, and Asclepiades of Bithynia, the Father of Molecular Medicine." *Vivo* 23 (2009): 507–14.

Acknowledgments

I COULD NOT HAVE WRITTEN THIS BOOK WITHOUT the gentle, expert, and scrupulous psychiatric and medical help of therapists Julia Sleeper and Philippa Ridley and my G.P., Dr. Flora Bailey. Long ago my friends Cathy Williams, Charlie Rose, Fiona Macintosh, and the sorely missed Ewen Green got me through some very dark times. Peggy Reynolds told me, affectionately, that I had to write the book in the first place. Etta Chatterjee's doctoral research on suicide in Sophocles' *Ajax,* which I supervised, taught me more than I can express. Dr. Hanita Ritchie, Local History Officer at the John Gray Centre & East Lothian Libraries in Haddington, guided me to invaluable sources on my ancestors, as did Pauline Smeed of the Dunbar and District History Society. Richard Campbell kindly helped me track down the arresting image on the book's jacket, and Hardeep Dhindsa took the photograph, which is reproduced with his permission; I am also grateful to Alessandro Vatri for help with locating the original painting of *Farewell to Socrates by His Wife Xanthippe.* My father, Stuart Hall, died in 2023 while the book was being prepared for publication. The year before, he had opened up to me for the first time about some details of my grandmother's funeral. My brother Walter Hall's support of the whole family during the final years of our father's life was selfless. Nicky and Andy Nicholson furnished practical assistance; my second cousins Jane Moore and Barbara Moore provided photographs, memories, candid discussion, and invaluable moral encouragement. Jane's daughter Hannah Parry, Paul Cartledge, Matt Shipton, Margarethe Debrunner, and Marina Carr all read early drafts and offered suggestions, corrections, or cheer in generous measure. Heather Gold at Yale University Press welcomed the project and has provided sterling support at every stage. Susan Laity has been a meticulous copyeditor. But my most profound debts are to the consistent sympathy and humor of Frances, Sarah, and Georgie Poynder and to their father, my stalwart, loyal, kind, and quick-witted husband, Richard Poynder. He has aided and sustained me in every way—driving me to archives, cemeteries, and ancestral haunts, researching genealogies and addresses, taking most of the photographs in the book, talking through issues, keeping me company during the Covid-19 lockdown and in the face of serial problems both in my working life and with my health and that of our children. He also makes the best cup of tea in Britain.

◇ ◇ ◇

This is the text of the blog I wrote, with further family photographs, in response to my father's death, at https://edithorial. blogspot.com/2023/06/goodbye-to-my-father-man-of-god.html.

Like Shakespeare, Raphael and Ingrid Bergman, my father, the Reverend Professor Stuart George Hall, died yesterday on his birthday, 7 June. He had just completed 95 years alive. Given his age, his visible deterioration over the last few months and our troubled relationship, I am amazed at how winded I feel.

Born to a working-class East London couple, a police constable and a seamstress, he ascended via scholarships at UCL School and Oxford to a firm niche in the Middle Class. My feelings about him are complicated. We did not rub along temperamentally, or rather, were not able to discover if we might have done had we not disagreed about many important issues. He was the type of man who was loved by all outside the household—his academic colleagues, students and parishioners—but found it hard to be an emotionally supportive father.

Growing up in a nuclear family where all decisions need to be referred to an invisible Almighty, whose views are relayed by his vicarious male agent on earth, is a weird experience. When I lost all belief in the Christian faith at the age of 13, my father was incandescent.

He was not a supporter of feminism (I recall his opposition to the Equal Pay Act 1970). He found it almost impossible to express any pride in my achievements (I cannot speak for my siblings). He was slow to anger, but his infrequent outbursts of rage were terrifying. He was no domestic democrat, and was absolutely furious when in my teens I began addressing everyone in the family as "Citizen."

I did have it out with him after our mother died in 2016. Although he did not apologise, he acknowledged that he could have made much more of an effort to be supportive. Our recent last meeting, attended by his new wife and my husband, entailed real, affectionate communication and was, I am glad to say, unprecedentedly warm and friendly.

And there are many things I owe to him, besides a firm jawline and an absurdist sense of humour.

He never embraced bourgeois values and when tired started to sound a little like the East-End boy he had been. Childhood interactions with his large circle of working-class relatives irrevocably shaped my politics. He hated racism and I was absolutely inspired at about the age of ten when he rebuked some distant relatives from the Texas Bible belt who had used derogatory language about African Americans.

He had a great sense of fun when he allowed himself to express it, and composed hilarious poems to divert his children when things were boring (as they often were in the 1960s). We used to drive all the way to Scotland at least three times a year. I adored his epic about Romans on Hadrian's Wall, of which, sadly, I can only remember four lines, with deliberately tortuous rhymes:

> Send us the Scots and we will fight 'em.
> We are stationed at CorstopItum.

Send us the Picts and we will fix 'em.
We are stationed half a mile from Hexham.

He loved cats and we had long, jokey conversations, which I remember almost daily, about what different tail shapes and positions might signify. He was the best shoe-shiner in history, and I can polish black leather boots to a radiant gloss.

I learned how to give a decent lecture by comparing his riveting sermons with those by the usual verbose and uncharismatic C of E preachers. Never more than ten minutes, a simple, lucid argument, improvised without any notes; sustained eye contact and clear diction, at least one joke and always a ringing quotation from the best prose in the King James Bible. It is down to him also that I know most of the Old Testament backwards.

He taught me my first steps in Greek by helping me decode the first sentence of John's gospel and explained why "Beginning" had no definite article. His own academic publications set a lofty bar on clarity, elegance and meticulous scholarship that I have tried hard to emulate.

I am so completely my father's daughter that I feel intense sadness at the many things that kept us apart emotionally. That is my sincere final message to him, if he can hear me after death, as, in his piety, he was convinced he would be able to forever.

Index

Index

Index

Index

Index

Index